Confessions
OF A DANCER

EMILY SOPHIE

This edition is published by
That Guy's House in 2019

www.ThatGuysHouse.com

Hey,

Welcome to this wonderful book brought to you by That Guy's House Publishing.

At That Guy's House we believe in real and raw wellness books that inspire the reader from a place of authenticity and honesty.

This book has been carefully crafted by both the author and publisher so that it will bring you hope, inspiration and sensation of inner peace.

It is our hope that you thoroughly enjoy this book and pass it onto somebody who may also be in need of a glimpse into their own magnificence.

Have a wonderful day.

Love,

Sean Patrick

That Guy.
www.ThatGuysHouse.com

BOOK LOVE

"Emily does all performers a great service by sharing her raw story and giving profound techniques for moving through challenge with ease. Confessions of a dancer is a must read for anyone wanting to reach their potential and avoid burnout"

-Tara Stiles, Founder of Strala Yoga

"Emily speaks in such a loving way and so easy to relate to. This book could change your life forever!"

-Mel Wells, Bestselling Author, Speaker, Actress

"Emily's work of inspiring women to create a strong, respectful mindset is refreshing in a world where comparison and self-loathing is the norm. A book filled with personal stories and action steps to make real change"

**-Emma and Carla Papas,
AKA The Merrymaker Sisters**

"Honest, powerful and inspiring"

-Chio, Broadway Dance Center Faculty, International Choreographer

"Emily is open and honest about the reality of how trying dance training can be, physically and most importantly mentally. I think every budding professional dancer should have this on their bedside table. I wish this book had been available when I was at dance college; finding the balance between the strenuous training and practicing self-love would have definitely changed the experience I had"

-Cat Sandion, CBeebies Presenter, Performer

"This is a great look into the life of Emily and her career as a performer. Such a brave step and honest view into the mind of a creative. An insightful book tackling mental health, confidence and self-worth with some lovely helpful tips along the way"

-Jamie Body, Presenter, Performer, Entertainment Correspondent

For my parents, sister and John-my greatest teachers

And for everyone out there following their dreams

TABLE OF CONTENTS

INTRODUCTION

It has taken well over a decade to learn the lessons I have, to get me to a place where I now *choose* to live in the light and magic of life and I want to show you just *how* I did it, so you too, can join me on the other side.

And what's in store for you on the other side?

Freedom and a whole load of love.

Life is *meant* to be an adventure filled with all the good things that we know and love and the way to create this as our reality, is *always* by learning to love *ourselves* unconditionally first.

I now make it my priority to practice being my own best friend and giving myself the love and care I deserve every single day, because I know that when I do this, I am stepping into my spotlight and shining the light that was always meant to be seen.

But I wasn't always this way...

When I first started dance college, I entered what I'm going to call my own 'Dark Ages', where I was *constantly* searching for the light of life, grasping at happy wisps whenever I could, only to feel my grip lessen each time as they always seemed to float out of my hand and I was left feeling downtrodden and disappointed time and time again.

At this point in my life, I was depressed, anxious and desperate to feel connected and worthy in myself. I was also in a full time professional Performing Arts College that tested me to my *very* core and provided me with a lifetime of lessons, squashed down into three intensive years.

I struggled for *so long* thinking that life and the emotions I experienced were simply 'out of my control' and just 'always going to be there' and felt there really was *nothing* I could do to change that.

I had convinced myself that it was *other* people and *outside* circumstances who were actually *causing* my unhappiness and pain and that I was sure I needed the *same two things* to pull me out of my darkness.

I was paralysed with fear, just trying to make it through each day, barely even living, never *mind* thriving.

My soul felt crushed, my heart was heavy and I carried around a *lot* of hurt and pain for years, simply because I thought there wasn't any other way to release myself from my negative state.

That and I was *still* waiting for that *one* person or thing to come and save me.

As you read on, you will learn that *we* are the ones here to save ourselves.

We are here to *connect, respect* and *honour* ourselves.

And we are the *only* people in control of our lives, because we are the *only* ones in control of our emotions, thoughts and actions.

I believe it is our greatest job and journey in life, to learn how to love ourselves *exactly* as we are, so that we can experience life as the *best* version of ourselves possible and allow *all* of the magic to enter into our realities.

Life *wants* to give us everything we desire.

Life *wants* us to win.

Life *wants* to show us the magic and light.

And it's only *us* who get in the way of that.

Changing your life and how you feel is *always* available to you in any given moment, because you *always* have a choice of how you want to create your reality.

I got extremely used to the 'reaction first, think later' method that my reality was always *far* from what I wanted it to be.

When I realised that *no one* was coming and that *nothing* in the future *would* or *could* make me happy if I wasn't already in that state in the present moment, I finally let go and decided to move *with* the flow of life, rather than against it.

I started taking responsibility for myself *and* my life and actively began creating my reality, just the way I wanted it to be.

I had given myself the greatest gift.

A chance at being the person I knew I had always been *deep* down.

An opportunity to thrive and enjoy my life.

And the knowledge that *I* was the one I'd been waiting for.

YOU are your own gift and *you* hold all the power inside you to feel happy, joyous, excited, empowered, confident and worthy.

And *so* much more.

This is the book I most needed to read in my darkest hour; it's the one with *all* the answers I was so desperately looking for and it's filled with my confessions of everything I've learned since waking up to the secrets of life. Which incidentally, are *always* available for the taking at any moment once we become aware of them.

If you're searching for a way out of the darkness, keep reading.

The light is most *definitely* at the end of the tunnel and it is my hope that you take less time to dig your way out than I did!

I have shared everything I know, in the hope that whoever needs to hear it, will.

CHAPTER 1

SELF-LOVE...AND WHY WE NEED IT IN BUCKET LOADS

The term 'self-love' has really done the rounds in recent years.

People are hash tagging and shouting about it all over the place.

But what does it *really* mean?

When I was in dance college, I had never even heard of this term, so clearly didn't follow its principles or message and of course, why would I?

I hadn't got a clue it even existed.

Then when the term started crazing the online world, I noticed it more and more and wondered what the hell it all meant.

For years, I thought I had 'got it' when really, I was part of the many who just used it in a sentence without really understanding the full meaning OR choosing to live by its message daily.

Growing up, I was horrifyingly shy. I mean, like the shyest person you can think of...I was *that* girl.

I never went to parties without my mum coming too, even at playschool my mum was one of the volunteers and I wouldn't leave her side.

It took me *years* before I wanted to go to sleepovers, only to get my dad to pick me up really early the next day in case I didn't like being away on my own.

I wouldn't talk to new people without having someone by my side coaxing the words out of me; it made me utterly anxious when my sister asked me to visit her in France when I was twelve and I'd have to go on a plane alone...so I didn't go.

I never talked to boys and got hot sweats and a thumping in my chest if one of them even *looked* at me and I *never* put myself forward in dance classes for fear of standing out and being judged.

So, to sum up, I was a delicate little shell of a person, afraid of basically everything.

Everything, except being on stage (and no the irony is not lost on me) and being around my family and *really* close friends (even staying with my grandparents was out of the question if it meant I'd have to go alone!).

So, I created a nook, a little haven and my ultimate comfort zone.

It felt safe, warm and cosy and I had all the love I needed forever more.

But then I grew up and we moved away from my lovely childhood home in East Yorkshire to Cambridge...where everyone spoke funny and thought *I* was the one with the weird Northern accent.

It was at *this* time that I began to realise that my nook wasn't a nook anymore, but a scary, new alien land that was demanding me to fit in when I felt I just *didn't* belong there.

Up until the age of ten (before we moved) I didn't need to worry about myself (as most children don't) because my family: mum, dad, older brother and sister, were always on hand to help me out, give me extra big doses of love and support and tell me everything was going to be okay if I ever had a wobbly.

But then after moving from 'Up North' to the South of England, leaving my friends, my old life and my safe comfort zone behind, I began to find life harder.

Which of course is to be expected when you start growing up.

It was now time to rely on myself a bit more, which was something I found I actually wasn't all that good at.

I used to seek out other people's approval, advice and opinions, never trusting my own judgement.

I listened to what *other* people thought I should and shouldn't do, more than listening to myself and I put A LOT of expectations on other people to make me feel happy, loved and safe.

As I got older and just before I left for dance college, I started to feel a bit more confident in myself (still no boyfriend to make me happy though of course…!) and found that I enjoyed being more independent (I'm talking trips into town and driving to my friend's house ten minutes down the road- but hey, you've got to start somewhere right) and actually *liked* having my own space.

I was all set for college, ready to 'leave the nest' and spread my wings.

I was really excited to do something I loved every, single day and I felt like I was probably going to be okay in this new dance environment, as *I* was always the one to be picked for solos, main parts in the shows, always put at the front and was chosen to help at my dance school as a part time job from a young age (a very prestigious role, I can tell you).

I thought I was all set.

Other people had told me I'd do great; my parents believed in me, my brother and sister were cheering me on and they never doubted my talents or abilities and all of my friends were proud of my achievement for getting into such a great college too.

So, you can imagine my shock and surprise after my first Ballet class at college (with the scariest Ballet Mistress I've *ever* been taught by-I actually used to get heart palpitations before entering the studio she was *that* terrifying) when I realised I was quite out of my depth and no longer a big fish in a little pond where everyone was on my side, bolstering me, guiding me and choosing me to be 'the favourite'.

This was hard.

Really hard.

And no one was molly coddling me now. I felt lost without my support group of family, friends and my safe little dance school.

I found my three years in training, the *hardest* of my life.

Now don't get me wrong, there were some really great times (mostly outside of college hours though) and I made amazing friends for life there.

But what made it hard for me was this…

I was reliant on other people to make me a) feel good b) tell me I was good enough and c) shower me with praise and love every day.

From my very lovely but sheltered upbringing, I was *so* dependent on outside circumstances and people to provide me with *everything* I needed and when they failed to do so, I became despondent and depressed and thought something was wrong with me because I was never consistently happy or felt fully in control of my emotions.

If I had known then what I know now, perhaps college would have been a very different experience for me (as I'm sure it was for those girls and guys who *had* their act together) but the truth is, unless you know...how can you know? You know?

So, coming back to this term 'self-love'...

I believe that *everything* starts and ends with this. It is probably *the* most important thing in our world if you want to be a happy, healthy, amazing human being.

It enables you to see the magic in life.

To live as if everything is a wonderful miracle.

To have this glow about you that just radiates out for all to see.

And it gives you EVERYTHING you've ever wanted; connection, joy, happiness, freedom, fun, fulfilment and of course the big one, love.

When we love ourselves, otherwise known as 'being our own best friend', all the negativity we feel, kind of just vanishes. It's like something amazing happens to our outer world *and* everyone in it.

Things don't faze you as much, people aren't as annoying, everything is a blessing or a lesson and stress no longer resides inside you.

Everything comes together and *you* create your own reality that's everything you've always dreamed of.

When we practice self-love, we begin the best relationship of our lives. WE become our own soul mates and 'the one'. It's all down to us and always has been.

When we learn to love ourselves, no one can ever have power over our joy or happiness, because this is something *we* create and generate daily.

There's a beautiful quote that my mum told me when I was much younger (that obviously was just sitting, waiting in the back of my mind until more recent years when I was ready to hear it) that says:

"No one can make you feel inferior without your consent" -Eleanor Roosevelt

I love this quote because it just about sums up everything about self-love and creating your own happiness.

We are *always* in charge of our realities, we choose this each and every day. We choose how we want to feel, even if we're not aware of it and our thoughts, emotions and actions have consequences either way.

If I heard a negative comment hurled at me from a teacher at dance college, that would have *utterly* broken me back then. I would have believed every word they said, let the hurt fester for days and feel rubbish about myself, because in my mind, *they* had just affirmed that I was in fact, not good enough after all.

But do you see that *I* chose how I reacted to that situation? If I had been practicing self-love and filled my cup to the overflow setting, then a comment like that wouldn't have phased me for long or even at all, because I would *know* that what *I* thought and believed about myself was *all* that truly mattered and that no one could *make* me unhappy, because *I* was the sole caregiver of all good things to myself.

Now I know what you must be thinking, "What if you receive a compliment or something positive is said to you?", well of course we all love to hear nice things about ourselves...we are human after all.

But the difference is, when you practice self-love and truly know that *you* are the only one who controls your own happiness, the compliment will be well received but not a necessity for you to feel happy and loved.

When we let go of our need for other people to bring us joy, love, connection or fulfilment, a magical thing happens.

We find true freedom.

Because no one person, place or thing can give you what YOU need.

You have to do that for yourself every, single day, for the rest of your beautiful life.

And when we *do* let go and love ourselves *this* fiercely, we are then able to love others even more than we ever thought possible, because our own cup of love is overflowing and that means we now have more than enough to share with others.

It's a lot of pressure to put on someone when we look to others to make us happy or give us love or any other positive emotion we wish to feel.

Which is why, relationships/friendships/any interactions with other beings, work so much better when both people are full up to bursting with all the good, positive emotions and feelings letting them give from *their* overflow, rather than always relying on the other person to give them what they are craving deep down.

The truth is, they will never quite manage it and you will always be left disappointed over and over again. Going around in circles, thinking you're crazy because you can't sustain a good feeling unless you have constant validation, love and approval from others.

By putting all of *my* demands for love, approval and validation on my teachers and peers at college, I was *constantly* frustrated all the time and I couldn't work out for the life of me, just *why* I was so miserable!

Every day I'd pray for someone to notice me, to get picked or complimented or told I was good enough, but even when those things *did* happen...I would be lit up for a short amount of time and then eventually crash, because at the end of the day...*I* didn't believe it was true.

I still felt unworthy, not good enough and constantly comparing myself with everyone else.

It was exhausting.

I (subconsciously) wanted other people to dictate my state and this is something that no other person can ever, ever do.

Until you learn that YOU are going to be the one to save yourself...you'll never be taken ashore and instead, you'll continue to live in the water, floundering and constantly waiting for someone else, who is (unfortunately) never going to come and rescue you.

I'm going to assume you've seen the film, Shrek...you know, the big green Ogre who's really a softy on the inside?

Well, if you've seen it, then you'll of course know of Princess Fiona (the feisty red head who's waiting for her Prince to come and save her from the Dragon in her tall tower and make all of her dreams come true).

Well, not to be a plot spoiler but…as it turns out, Princess Fiona has been cursed and turns into an Ogre at night (which Shrek doesn't find out until the end of course).

But the point is, Princess Fiona is waiting for true love's kiss to *make* her happy and turn her into a 'full time' beautiful Princess (by other people's standards) and when true loves kiss happens (by Shrek) she instead, becomes a 'full time' Ogre.

Princess Fiona is flummoxed and immediately saddened by her surprising transformation, but soon realises that who she *really* is and what she *believes* isn't dependent on someone else *making* her look or feel a certain way, because she has *and* will always have everything she needs inside her and this isn't dependent on her marrying a King or looking like a stereotypical Princess, or even kissing her true love.

She is everything, just by being herself and remembering that fact.

The same goes for you. And *everyone* on this planet.

We are all unique and we are *all* here to share that uniqueness with the world.

Our job is to practice loving ourselves first, so that the person we share with the world and everyone we love in it, is the best possible version we can be.

Mind, Body, Soul Love:

1. Become your own best friend. Treat yourself the way you love and care for your very best friend. Speak kindly to yourself, believe in yourself, accept yourself and know that you are worthy right now, just as you are.

2. Take care of you. Fill yourself up with nourishing food and respect your body like it's the only one you'll ever get...because it is. You are your home, so make it a lovely place to be.

3. Fill up your soul-feed yourself with positive, fulfilling, purposeful activities, people and experiences, so you become the very best version of yourself.

4. Always remember that YOU are responsible for your life. YOU create your own happiness, joy, love, fulfilment and freedom, because YOU are in charge of designing your own reality and your reactions to things and no one has power over you to 'make you' feel anything less than you desire.

CHAPTER 2

YOU ARE NOT A BROKEN RECORD...
YOU DO *NOT* NEED FIXING

Let me start by just saying this one very simple thing...you do not, I repeat, *do not* need fixing, because you are a) not broken and therefore b) there is nothing 'wrong' with you.

Right, now we've got that sorted, let me now tell you all the ways I tried to ignore this advice and stick myself back together, even though nothing was ever falling off.

A dancer's role is to be perfect. You are expected to always have perfect turn out, a perfect bun, a perfect pirouette and landing; you are supposed to be the perfect weight, size and shape, to always be perfect in everything you do. I could go on, but I won't because, well you're reading this book so you obviously *get it* already.

This high expectation on young minds, can lead to one believing that they are perhaps *not* perfect, because they are in fact, a human and humans are flawed and perfectionism does not actually exist and is therefore, not attainable.

And what comes then?

Well, a whole load of denial and thinking that you can dupe the system and find a loop hole that allows you to be this picture of perfection anyway and I can safely say, that this doesn't ever work (for reasons why, please re-read the paragraph prior).

So, what we have now is a dancer who is trying to be perfect, who can't *ever* achieve this goal (because deep down they *know* it doesn't exist) but continues each and every day to have another go at it because it is expected and *demanded* of them and maybe today will be different and they will be granted some relief...but always to no avail I might add.

I know, it's a cruel cycle and one I'm sure you can relate to.

And I got stuck inside this loop for *years*.

I tried my very best day after day to strive for this unattainable misconception, but each time I was given a critical comment, I felt my self-esteem go one notch lower and my energy for trying, even lower than that.

And each time I was complimented, I felt like I *still* wasn't good enough anyway, because there would always be a "...but next time try..." that followed.

Take countless years of this repetition and it's enough for anyone to go bonkers right!

As Einstein said *"Insanity is doing the same thing over and over again, but expecting different results"* and this was *definitely* an insane approach.

To keep striving for something that you know *has* never and *will* never exist? Equals, crazy times a million, right?

So, after years of going around in circles, you can imagine that this takes a bit of a toll on a person and may even cause a person to feel like there's something wrong with them because they just aren't able to achieve this *one tiny thing* with any success. Ever.

Then it struck me like lightening.

I'd got it in my head that if I could just 'fix' that one thing in me that was broken or wrong, everything would fit into place perfectly (yes, I did use that word on purpose).

So, I tried everything (and I mean *everything*), sometimes I didn't even know *why* I was doing that thing or what symptoms I'd actually gone to an appointment for, which now seems even crazier.

But I did it all anyway, again to no avail or relief.

No big surprise there.

I went to see multiple hypnotherapists because family members and friends had been and got great results for fear of flying or other phobias, but I didn't actually know *why* I was showing up or what I needed help with, I just needed someone to help fix whatever wasn't working in me.

And after countless sessions...no joy there.

Then I went for acupuncture...to sound/energy healing... spoke to a CBT specialist...no, no and no again.

I tried dying my hair...bought new clothes...tried new make-up...went paleo for a week...saw a psychic...I even tried changing my contraceptive pill to see if that would somehow miraculously change me into who I knew I could be and guess what...nothing, nada.

Then I went to the doctor and they put me on anti-depressants which actually *did* help relieve some of the pain I felt, only to bring it all back tenfold when I decided to come off them a year later.

And why didn't any of these things work?

Because I hadn't dealt with the *real* block underneath...my emotions that had been stored up over the years and created all of this anxiety and stress over the thought that I needed (and was expected) to always be perfect.

I had never addressed the real causes of *why* I was so unhappy and unfulfilled.

And the thing was, I knew this all along.

I knew what I'd gone through, I knew the things that kept me up at night and what I woke up worrying about each morning.

I knew all the things that *still* caused me hurt and pain that I'd never worked on releasing or clearing.

I hadn't done the inner work on myself, *by* myself first.

I remember hearing that for the first time and then, for the hundredth time and thinking "Yeah, I'm totally doing that" and then in the next thought thinking "Well, why isn't this working for me?", without actually realising that what I had been doing was still searching outside of myself when what I *really* needed to do was just to go inwards for a little while and pour some love into myself.

Like a lot of love.

Every single day.

If you're reading this and have experienced a similar thing or maybe find yourself in the middle of this uncomfortable process right now, then I urge you to go inwards and take some time to start there first.

Even though it feels hard and icky, even though it's the thing you *don't* want to do and even though, it feels like there will never come a day when you'll feel okay...keep going because that day is coming much sooner than you think if you stick with this, rather than constantly looking outside yourself for the answers. You will never, ever find them there. It's a pain and a cliché I know, but no one can do this but *you*.

I've said it before and I'll say it again, just to make sure it *really* goes in...you are *not* broken and do *not* need fixing.

You just might not be feeling quite yourself right now or maybe you didn't in the past and that's completely normal and okay and all you have to do to feel good again is trust that *you* and only *you* can pull yourself through to the other side.

Trust that you and *only* you have all the answers ready and waiting for you to tap into when you actually realise your own power.

And when you do, you'll see it really *is* all big fluffy white clouds, rainbows and unicorns...or maybe just beautiful white horses that sparkle (like unicorns).

Mind Love:

1. Write down all the things that still play on your mind/memories that feel negative to you when you think about them-keep listing each one until your mind is empty.

2. Now take each one in turn and change the scene. For example: something that played on my mind and caused me a lot of pain was when my Ballet teacher said in the middle of a Pas De Deux class "Emily, you have about as much passion as a lemon" and I was completely humiliated in front of all of my peers and that comment stayed with me for years after.

3. So, to clear this block that was *still* causing me pain, I decided to add comedy to the memory which changed the scene and my perception of it. I decided to *only* visualise my Ballet teacher and all of the other dancers present in the scene, in puffy lemon outfits with little hats on! Now, if that memory ever pops up, I only ever see the new image and I have a little chuckle to myself.

4. It sounds almost *too* simple, but I promise you it works. Our minds are *very* powerful and *very* susceptible and although we can never change what's happened to us, we can always change how we look back on that memory and turn it into something positive, so it no longer causes us pain.

5. The way you release negativity or negative memories/ thoughts/emotions, can differ from person to person. I like to add comedy to my negativity because it helps lighten the situation and makes me laugh, which to me, feels like the ultimate release.

6. But perhaps comedy isn't for you-perhaps you might like to put yourself back in the scene and tell the younger you everything you needed to hear at the time. Give the younger you all the love, support and hugs they need until you can finally let go of the hurt and pain.

7. Or maybe it might work better for you to see the scene as if you're watching it on a big cinema screen; you see yourself in the scenario and then you change it. For example, you could make the picture really big, then shrink it really small and then let it break into a million tiny pieces, or turn it from colour to black and white, mute it, slow it down, pause it, then smash the picture with a hammer...there are multiple ways of letting go here.

8. It can take a few goes to see what works best for *you* and this might be different each time you clear something, but you'll know if it's worked, because there won't be any emotion attached to the negative scene/ event or thought anymore and you'll feel, free.

CHAPTER 3

ONE PERSON'S OPINION, IS *NOT* GOSPEL

*"Don't let someone else's opinion
of you become your reality"*
- Les Brown

This quote just about sums up this whole chapter in ten words. Re-read it again before we move on and really comprehend what he's saying here.

I love this quote *so* much because it reiterates that we don't have to become what others think about us. We have the power to reinvent ourselves, to know that what *we* believe about ourselves is *way* more important than what anyone else believes about us and that we can create *any* reality we want for our lives.

If you're in the dance industry, then I'm sure you'll be familiar with the word "No" or a variation of it, like perhaps "You're just not what we're looking for", "Next", "Thank you for your time", "You're really talented, but your look just isn't 'us'" and finally "We really appreciate you coming down today, but unfortunately...".

I do sometimes wonder if it's actually a person's job to find a million different ways of rejecting someone so the people doing the rejecting can 'let them down easy' with a choice of phrases they pick from a spreadsheet...

But the truth is, any form of "No" is still a rejection and it hurts. A lot.

Sometimes, you may even shed a few tears because you wanted that job so badly and you just can't fathom why you didn't make it through...I know I felt like this almost every, single time I auditioned and I started to get really sick of being disappointed all the time.

After a while, I felt myself resenting the audition process (whereby at one time, I had actually really *loved* going) and so I kept on getting those ever hurtful "No" responses, again and again. And again.

One of the reasons I felt *so* saddened by my string of rejections, was that it felt like a personal attack on *me*.

Dancing is one of the few professions, where you are more judged on how you *look* over how you *perform technically* as to whether you'll fit their line-up and get the job.

So naturally it's easy to take offence when you don't get a role, because it feels like what they're really saying when they 'let you down gently' is "You're not good enough" and there develops the complex that begins to rule your life.

I suppose auditioning is like running a race.

You start with loads of energy; your heart is pounding with adrenaline and you have determination in your eyes.

You are focused, move easily and pick up your pace.

Other people are around you, but you stay in your own lane, eyes fixed on the end goal.

And then, as you approach the finish line, your feet feel stuck in the ground and you can't move beyond where you are, whilst those around you sprint eagerly past.

You want it so desperately and yet you never seem to cross the line.

Then you're left with a little less determination, a little less energy and a little less passion the next time you try.

This cycle seemed to continue to go downhill for me over the years and I wallowed in the fact that (in my eyes) *other people* were determining my future career and my general disposition and *not* me.

And that brings me back to this wonderful Les Brown quote we started with.

The only way I was allowing other people to determine my path, was because I *let* them.

I chose to believe *their* opinions over my own.

I chose to stay stuck in this cycle and not place my trust and belief in myself, where it truly belonged.

When I finally came to and realised this, things started to change for me and I began to take matters into my own hands.

I started creating my own opportunities and I changed my mindset to match my new, positive beliefs about myself and what I could *really* achieve in my life.

When I was stuck in the rejection cycle, I never realised how much of a role *I* was actually playing in keeping myself stuck in this continuum of constant "Noes".

You see, rejection can actually be a really good thing.

Now before you stop reading, let me explain and do it fast before I lose you for good!

When we get rejected from an audition, or anything for that matter, we are really being *redirected* to something else... something better.

Still with me?

Because on some level, you will not have been aligned with said audition in some way or another and therefore you didn't get it because you weren't energetically matched.

When I first learned this, I couldn't (didn't want to) believe it, because there had been times when I had gone for jobs that I wanted with all my heart...or so I thought.

But when I started to *really* analyse my emotions regarding these jobs, it appeared that maybe I wasn't *totally* in love with the idea of attaining them after all.

For example; a few years after graduating, I got a call to go for a *very* intimate, *very* last-minute audition for Cabaret (they were starting rehearsals the following week for their UK tour). When I put the phone down I was elated-it's not every day the tables are turned and *your* presence is requested at an audition.

This was it, I thought to myself as I ran to tell my parents the good news. My big break had finally come!

So, I went along (my body fired up with nerves) and had a very successful audition...until the end. Now, having not seen Cabaret before and clearly not having done any prior research, I didn't realise that for some of the show, cast members are required to be naked.

And I mean *totally* naked. Like everything out for all to see, live on stage, night after night. Even when your parents and nanny come to watch you.

Naked.

They reassured us that it was tasteful and necessary to the storyline, but as they were speaking my heart was pounding and, in that moment, I'd already subconsciously chosen my fate no matter how good my audition was and no matter how badly I *supposedly* wanted the job.

I didn't want to do it. But at the same time, I wanted this *so* badly. It was a fight between my head and my heart, fear and love and my subconscious and conscious mind.

They said if we were uncomfortable with being naked on stage, that was absolutely fine, but we had to tell them there and then so they could not include us in the final decision.

But I literally could not move.

Plus, everyone else seemed to be really cool about it as no one said a word, so I just pretended I was too and joined the silenced crowd by doing and saying nothing (which wasn't hard seeing as I appeared to have lost all control over my body at this point).

They told us they would call later that day as they needed to confirm the final member of the cast ASAP. So, when I heard my phone buzz a few hours after the audition and heard that all too familiar variation of "No" rejection down the line, I felt crushed and relieved all at the same time.

No matter *how* much I had wanted that job, there was always a part of me that would actually stop me from getting it, because my emotions around performing naked were *so* negatively ingrained and strong, that my mind had to obey and listen to the more powerful voice inside (my subconscious) that didn't want to be told "Yes" and to actually have to go through with being *so* outside my comfort zone.

This might all sound a little far-fetched at first, but our minds are capable of extraordinary things. Believe me.

We always have to be on the same frequency of what it is that we want and *really* believe that we a) *truly* want it deep down and b) deserve it and believe we can achieve it, to in fact get it.

As you can see, I may have thought I desperately wanted this coveted role, but in actual fact, subconsciously I didn't because my fear far outweighed the love for it and so my frequency did not match that of the job and the result...I got rejected.

BUT...redirected to something that was more in line with me at that time.

The mind will always give you what you think about most. Add to this a strong emotion and you can almost guarantee that your wish/fear will come true, as mine did with my fear of performing in the nuddy!

Remember when I said that over time I began to resent the audition process? Well I also began to have thoughts like this:

"I know I won't get it"

"*Why* am I even here?"

"I should have just stayed at home"

"Those girls are so much better than me"

"I hate feeling like this"

"I don't even want to try because I know I won't be what they want"

And so on...

Now, as you're becoming more aware that your thoughts have a *huge* effect on your reality, you can imagine what kind of vibration I was working with here right?

It was self-sabotage on *so* many levels and I just didn't want to stop myself, because being proven right (and hearing

"No") was more satisfying than actually getting a part and having to admit that *I* was wrong about what I thought was the industry's unfair selection process.

When we actually take the time to get clear on what it is *we* want, rather than what we think we *should* want, we align ourselves with roles and opportunities that *really* speak to us and as a result, we are fully invested, believe we can achieve it and believe we deserve it and are therefore, more likely to fulfil our desires.

When I decided to go after what I really wanted, the seas parted and everything fell into place for me. It was a whole new experience and one that I found was working much better than the one I had participated in for so many years prior.

I began to listen to my intuition, rather than anything outside myself.

I began to trust that *I* knew what I wanted and I began to create things for myself because it felt good to step up and make what I wanted happen in reality.

Mind Love:

When you rock up to an audition or job interview in the future thinking that the panel are the ones who hold your fate in their hands...think again and make sure you check yourself first.

Ask yourself the following questions:

1. Do I *really* want this?

2. Am I *totally* aligned with it?

3. Do I *fully* believe that I can achieve this?

If you get three yeses, you're in! If not, then maybe ask yourself "Why not?" and really get to know the person facing the mirror and remember that your thoughts, beliefs and opinions are the only ones that *truly* matter.

CHAPTER 4

YOUR BODY, YOUR TEMPLE, YOUR HOME

As a dancer, the most important tool you have to express yourself creatively with, is your body.

It's what is going to bring in the dollar bills (not in a Pretty Woman kind of way I hope) and it is your greatest asset in this industry.

Which is why it is *so* important to take care of this vessel, if you want longevity in your career and to avoid getting injured and having to impatiently wait offside for months and months.

It's not a coincidence that people joke how a dancer's diet basically consists of 'Coca Cola and Kit Kats', because many dancers are actually not aware (because we're not taught) how to eat properly and what this *really* looks like in terms of meals on our plates, snacks in between classes and actually fuelling our bodies for energy to last throughout the day.

I remember a time in dance college when we were taking part in a body conditioning class (which mostly consisted of sit ups, more sit ups and oh yes, more sit ups) and our teacher felt compelled to share some of her 'healthy eating' wisdom by telling us that if we felt hungry, we were really just thirsty and should drink water and if we *really* had to eat, it should be an apple.

I listened through sweaty ears whilst obediently performing my hundredth sit up and wondered...could this advice really be true?

Luckily for me, I had always had great parents for role models who were all about eating well and exercising, plus I *loved* food and had always enjoyed the act of eating, so I chose to ignore this information and follow my own intuition instead.

Because as I said, I loved food too much to *only* ever eat apples and also because of my extremely fast metabolism, if I didn't eat regularly I'd feel faint, weak and like I was going to collapse.

But for some of my friends, I know that *this*, along with other comments about eating/implied weight loss, *really* affected them and eating disorders were not an uncommon thing to witness in our college...and in many others too I might add.

Now, I'm not totally faulting the advice we were given back then, because after all, the dance teachers imparting said advice weren't actually qualified to, so they only spoke of what *they* knew and passed that on to us with what they thought was 'good advice'.

But food *is* a vital part of a dancer's life and needs to be addressed so that our temple can remain strong and healthy inside, as well as out.

After college, I swotted up on nutrition because it was something I was *really* interested in and I was also on a mission to try and solve my mystery stomach issues that had been prevalent since aged fourteen.

So, I became a personal trainer/nutritional advisor and delved into the world of food and did my own further research trying and testing what felt good for my body and what didn't.

It's been an ongoing learning curve because each body is different and I've learned that no 'one way' of eating is the 'right way', but here are a few things that I believe can help maintain a healthy body for years to come and what I do my best to follow in my own life:

1. Eat more plants-mother nature has provided everything we need on this Earth and eating lots of plant-based food gives us more energy, a healthy digestive system, brighter/clearer skin and tastes really good too!

2. Drink a *lot* of water-this goes without saying for a 'normal' person, but for dancers, we sweat out a lot of fluid when dancing, so need to replenish these lost fluids to stay hydrated, energised and focused.

3. Avoid processed foods-yes, I'm afraid this means your local takeaway, because it's not doing your insides much good and will make you feel sluggish, play havoc with your hormones and we all know that uncomfortable bloated feeling it gives you afterwards...

4. Avoid refined sugar-this was a very hard one for me at college, as I saw it as a little pick me up, but the thing with refined sugar is, it picks you up-then it drops you down. So, instead try natural sugars if you need a little lift and your taste buds will soon start to change.

These are just a few general things that have really helped me to feel on top form, but as I said, each body is different, which is why learning to listen to your own body is such a *huge* thing, as it enables you to give yourself what *you* truly need to thrive.

This is a great time to stop and think about how your body *feels* when eating different foods too. I know how boring it can be to do a food diary, so don't worry, that's not on the cards today, but what I will say is to notice how your body reacts to certain food, what emotions are prevalent when you eat and what food *really* satisfies you.

Get to know yourself and food like a relationship and keep trying and testing different ways to see what works best, *for you*.

Keep it light and fun, because if you're stressing over food, then chances are lots of things won't sit well with you, which is *exactly* what I learned from my many, *many* years of stressing.

From the age of fourteen, I started noticing that my stomach was becoming increasingly more sensitive to a *lot* of different foods and having a fast metabolism already, well let's just say, I needed a little more meat on my bones. And this all started around the same time that I was bullied at school (not coincidently).

I spent years accepting that *this* was my new normal. Except, it didn't *feel* normal.

So, when I just wasn't happy to accept this state of being anymore, I started testing and trialling different foods and ways of eating, until I figured out just *what* was happening inside me.

After a whole lot of testing, I am now at a place where I understand my body (for the most part, some days it just likes to do its own thing...or if I get Bali belly...well that's a different story) and I know what makes me feel great and what doesn't and I choose the things that make me feel good because I know that *that's* the state I want to be in each day.

I also found on my food discovery that *stress* was an almighty player in my stomach issues and when I started to work on soothing my mind and clearing out the negativity, it in turn soothed my insides too.

Shocking, right?!

It's easy and convenient to choose grab and go food, especially when you have rehearsals, are rushing in between classes, travelling between working ten different jobs etc... but this grab and go lifestyle doesn't have to be all Coca Cola and Kit Kats.

There are *so* many options nowadays that enable *everyone* to make a healthier choice.

If you've got a busy schedule (I mean, who doesn't in this day and age) and proclaim that you *don't* have enough time to prep healthy snacks, remember this: Beyoncé has the same twenty-four hours that we all do...just saying.

Anyway, all jokes aside (although I'd never joke about Queen B) if you find yourself saying this more times than you can count, maybe take a look at the following time-consuming activities that could be better spent caring for your nutrition...which in turn takes care of your body...which in turn helps you have a longer, more sustainable career...

1. Scrolling through Facebook
2. Scrolling through your Instagram feed
3. Perfecting the 'perfect' selfie for the hundredth time
4. Binge watching Netflix
5. Snoozing
6. Staring into space

You see, you've already gained about twenty hours of your day back by cutting down on the above! Just think how many sweet potato coconut curries you could make in that time.

Again, all jokes aside, this stuff is important and *deserves* your time and attention, because the truth is, no one is going to do it for you (unless you hire a private chef, then I stand corrected).

Along with food, we obviously need to be aware of how we're moving our bodies too, as this is what will bring in the moolah each and every year as a dancer.

But another preconception that many people (including dancers) have, is that dancers are automatically healthy and strong just because they dance and are moving their bodies for the majority of the time.

As I have outlined above and through my own experience of being a chocoholic and sweetie fiend throughout my college days, this is *not* necessarily the case.

Dancers move their bodies in a very specific way, but we are also not usually told how to move in other, extremely beneficial ways too, like Pilates and Yoga for example.

I remember when I went to train at Broadway Dance Center in New York and decided it would be a good idea to try Pilates for the first time (I was twenty-five).

Those classes probably tested me more than *any* of my dance ones, because my body wasn't used to moving in that way so I had to create new muscle memory and it took a while for me to actually 'get it'.

What was shocking to me was that I couldn't actually do some of the exercises! I mean, I was a dance and fitness professional and I couldn't move my leg forward and backward whilst lying on my side without rolling over my hip and collapsing onto the floor?

Madness.

But over time, I created *new* strength that I had never had before and a core that was so rock solid that I felt invincible.

I craved this new way of moving, just as much as I craved my dance classes, because by doing Pilates, I was able to dance better too.

Let me explain: all movement comes from your core, so even if you dance, you may not have a strong core, so by working these muscles (not just by doing sit ups I might add) you can create a new strength that allows you to move easily from your centre and test your boundaries and comfort zone. This is because your body allows you to and you trust it more with supporting you in each step, jump, twist and turn.

It felt only natural then that I went to train as a Pilates Instructor and found that this form of exercise and movement was so complimentary to my dance practice that I needed to learn as much as I could to help myself and others to feel strong and confident in *their* bodies too.

And just in case you weren't aware, Joseph Pilates started this movement phenomenon to help with the rehabilitation of dancers' injuries.

It was actually *made* for dancers!

What's funny is that during my time at Broadway Dance Center, I also tried Yoga for the first time (because I'd sprained my ankle and couldn't do as much dancing during those months) and this again, was a completely *new* way of moving my body that I was definitely *not* used to.

To be really honest, I didn't like Yoga much back then-I felt like I was forcing my body into poses and I was intimidated by upside down moves and balancing in a handstand...so I avoided doing this at all costs and only when the teacher was looking, would I pretend to be working out the mechanics of how my body would get into these moves, without *ever* actually attempting them.

But fast forward a few years to the day I met Tara Stiles and my Yoga perception would change forever.

I was attending Be:Fit in London with two of my friends from college and I'd signed up to do a Yoga class (I was going in my leggings anyway so thought I'd better put them to good use) and the other two were signed up to different classes, so I went alone.

I was a little nervous as I have already let slip that I wasn't the *greatest* Yoga fan back then, also, I had never even *heard* of Tara Stiles before that day, so I didn't know what I was in for at all.

Before the class started, Tara, a tall, graceful woman with a great big smile came out to great us all, then we entered a room filled with what must have been about one hundred mats and the class began.

Music came out across the speakers playing...well it was playing almost soft rock and popular songs that I loved and this movement, well it was very different.

There was no pressure, no forcing and instead, there was moving with ease, with softness and how it felt good to move and I absolutely loved it!

I left the class feeling so inspired, energised and happy, that when I met my two friends, I had the biggest grin on my face and I think they thought I may have gone slightly mad in the time we'd been apart.

But I was hooked and I continued to follow her online Yoga classes regularly after that, telling anyone who would listen about her cool style *and* the fact that she too had been a dancer.

It only took me about three years to actually get up the courage to do her Strala Yoga Teacher Training, which was a fantastic experience and exactly what I needed at the time to deepen this practice and get really connected to myself.

Learning to move your body in a way that feels easy and good for you is a true blessing and one that gives you an extremely wonderful, natural high.

But to be able to do this and do it well, I had to let go of control and be okay with positions and movements *not* looking perfect (in my eyes) and this took a while to drop, as I was so used to striving for perfection.

But I'll always remember the feeling I got when I did-it was pure bliss and a new kind of elated feeling that I was extremely pleased to add to my dancing repertoire of natural highs.

As dancers, it is important to create a strong, healthy body that supports our passion of dance, so finding other ways of moving to aid this, is really helpful and ultimately, feels great too.

Body Love:

1. Make conscious choices for fuel...this means, when you grab something to eat, be aware of *how* it'll make you feel, is it what your body is *really* craving and will it nourish you in a way that feels good? Every time we eat, we have a choice, so start to listen to your body and choose according to what it tells you, because our bodies are smart-they know what they need to function at their best.

2. Strengthen your body so you can perform at your physical peak, without injury and gain even more longevity, by adding in Yoga and Pilates alongside your dance classes. A strong, supple body will aid you in your dance career and also help with your confidence, physical health and make everyday life feel easy and in flow.

CHAPTER 5

DON'T BELIEVE THE WHISPERS

I grew up always knowing that I wanted to dance.

That was a given and something I was certain of. It was a fact and *everyone* knew it.

I also grew up listening to the whispers from the dance industry and came to believe that everything I heard, was also fact, trusting them all implicitly without second guessing or doing any kind of counter research myself.

Unfortunately, my parents, siblings, friends and teachers all believed these whispers to be true too.

Perhaps you've also heard them?

"Dancer's don't make a lot of money"

"You've got to be in it for the love, not the money"

"You only have a few good years to dance"

"After thirty, you won't be able to perform anymore as you'll be too old"

"The industry is bitchy and mean"

"Your body will end up disfigured and your feet mushed from wearing Pointe shoes"

"You've ultimately failed if you *just* teach dance"

"Everyone gets the second-year blues in college"

"You've got to be ruthless and competitive to get anywhere"

"All dancers suffer with anorexia and eating disorders"

"You can't make proper friends in the industry, because they'll always be your competition"

And so on...

Any you recognise here?

The thing is, you don't even need to be a dancer to have heard these whispers about the dance industry.

It's seen as *fact* to everyone. Everyone who believes it to be true anyway.

But I'd like to challenge one or two, or in fact *all* of these 'statements' for their validity and supposed truth and I'd ask you to bear with me as I do my best to unravel this worldwide web of confusion and ultimately, false perception of the dance industry.

If we take the top one to start and dig a little deeper, you'll be able to see that perhaps it is a little, shall we say outdated and actually quite incorrect.

"Dancer's don't make a lot of money"

This is a worldwide well known 'fact' and yet there are dancers/choreographers/dance educators and teachers out there right now, making a great living from their craft.

By stating this to be true, it does five things:

1. It doesn't allow any room for questioning its validity and therefore is seen as fact which in turn you believe with all your heart to be true, no exceptions.

2. You unknowingly block any form of income from dancing that may perhaps offer you *more* than what is 'expected' for a dancer's salary, because your subconscious holds the above statement to be true

and is therefore protecting you against anything that may upset this belief.

3. Leaders/agents/employers in the industry take advantage of this 'fact' and offer artists well below what they deserve or sometimes even zero pay (we've all heard the "great exposure", "good experience" or "fantastic on your CV" lines right?) and because that is what 'is' in the industry, they are honouring this fact and we accept it and therefore take those jobs because we think that is *all* there is available to us and ultimately, it's *our* job so there's no other way around it if we want to be in work.

4. If we make *more* than what we expect from this industry, we may feel unworthy of the money, deceitful because it goes against the grain or even dirty for being the exception to this rule and somehow we will either lose, spend or dwindle it all away so we don't have to deal with feeling that way anymore so we can go back to playing the role already set out for us as a 'credible, struggling artist'.

5. This statement becomes a self-fulfilling prophecy and continues to be passed along the chain for generations to come.

This thought process and reality can be true of any of the above statements about the dance industry, or any thought we believe to be true, because the main point is, our minds will believe whatever we tell them the most.

I went into professional training with the mindset that I was following my dreams, but that they would ultimately cost me, because I wouldn't be able to make a stable living doing what I loved and as a result, I struggled for years.

But in my head, I was doing it 'for the love of it' so this *far* outweighed actually making money and being able to provide for myself...or so I convinced myself due to the already cemented belief that had been ingrained in my mind from a young age.

The funny thing is, that when I was actually earning a great wage for dance work, I somehow sabotaged this and ended up broke again because, my subconscious was trying to keep me safe and therefore stuck in my comfort zone where I could say I danced because I loved it and not because I wanted to make money from my passion.

Now I know what you're thinking, surely it doesn't feel very comfy to not have money to live independently or fully, but *that* part actually doesn't matter to the subconscious mind, because at the end of the day, it doesn't concern itself with those details-only the fact that by earning money and becoming financially independent and free, I was going against my established belief and therefore 'putting myself in danger' (out of my comfort zone) where things were different and could potentially cause me pain.

On the one hand it really doesn't make any sense why we're programmed to protect ourselves in this way, but of course way back when, it came in very useful when lions approached and we had to retreat into our comfort zones (caves) to stay safe and well.

But living in today's age, these things aren't really a daily concern for most of the population, so this is where retraining or reprogramming our minds comes in to play and why we *need* to do it in order to become our best selves and really thrive in life.

This is why some people feel stuck for years, because in their minds they're replaying and reliving the same old outdated beliefs, that don't really do much for their growth or development.

It's a vicious cycle if you're in it and easy to get back in once you're out, if you let yourself.

But when you start training your mind to think differently and create your *own* beliefs that actually help you to progress in life, then you're able to do things you never thought you once could…like make money from doing what you love *and* enjoy it at the same time.

If you allow your old limiting beliefs to continue to play out, then even if you prove yourself wrong, you'll somehow sabotage your greatness and match your reality to your old beliefs, staying stuck but also right about life and safely tucked up in your comfort zone.

This was my own reality *far* too many times to say, but after the millionth time of not learning a lesson and getting the same result, you kind of sit up and pay attention.

When I was twenty-two, I had already done various performing gigs as a dance professional, which were all amazing opportunities, so I tried my hand at teaching full time at a culture school in Norway where I would be earning £30k for the year, which totally blew my young, little mind at the time.

It was a fantastic experience, I made loads of great friends and loved what I did, but at the end of the year when it came to deciding whether I wanted to stay on for a full time position or not, I toiled away not knowing what to do.

I *loved* being in Norway, I loved my job, I loved that I was financially independent and I loved getting to hang with my best friend every day. But another part of me (the ego part and the one that likes to self-sabotage because it thinks it knows best) wanted to move back to London and try and 'make it as a dancer' again, even if that meant I'd be broke, because I'd be doing it for the love, not the money of course.

Are you getting it now?!

At the *very* last opportunity to decide my fate, I chose to move back to the UK and thus ended up spending another few years *just* scraping by, getting help from my parents and being miserable because I ultimately wasn't doing what I had come home to do.

My days were spent teaching classes I had to travel hours to, with students who this time, didn't actually *want* to be there and that paid very little, meaning that I couldn't attend auditions in the day and didn't have any excess money for classes in my spare time.

And guess what, my old belief that "dancers don't make a lot of money" came back tenfold and I had proved myself right yet again (despite earning £30k the year before doing what I loved) which gave me some satisfaction and let up for taking responsibility for my circumstances, because it wasn't *my* fault-it was just, fact.

Now rest assured, I'm not doing a blame train on myself, because most of the time I had no idea that I was even *thinking* like this. It's only after years of personal development and learning that I can look back and see what was going on beneath the surface.

Most of us would never consciously choose things that are going to hurt or cause us discomfort in one way or another, but subconsciously, it's a whole other story and one we're not aware of until, well, until we are.

As for the other statements at the beginning of this chapter, I have found very different outcomes when I started to change my mindset and beliefs.

For example:

When I turned thirty, I got more dance gigs than I had for years before and was in the best health and fitness I'd ever been in, proving that you're *never* too old to do anything if it's in your heart.

I have met *so* many wonderful dancers in my career, both as colleagues and as my students in class and made lifelong friends, who I know will always have my back and who *want* me to succeed and actively support me as much as they can, proving that the industry *isn't* as bitchy and mean as we've been told to believe.

My body has supported me every day of my life and continues to do so, because I move daily, eat well and treat it with respect. I get stronger with each year that passes and know that dancing my whole life has given me flexibility, ease of movement and a supportive frame that allows me to enjoy life fully, proving that your body *won't* become disfigured if you take care of it.

Some of the best moments in my career so far are when I have been in front of a class, teaching. I absolutely *adore* teaching dance and watching people grow and develop in front of my eyes. There's a special kind of reward you receive from teaching, when you know that a student (no matter how old or young) has allowed themselves to be truly vulnerable and overcome their self-doubt to walk out of the class, a more confident version of themselves, proving that *teaching* dance is *just* as valid as performing and is most definitely *not* a failure.

You get the idea.

What we tell ourselves constantly, has a *huge* impact on the reality we see before us each day.

So, if we have ingrained beliefs that we are *not* as good as everyone else in the industry, or *not* able to make a living from doing what we love, or that we *won't* make friends because everyone is apparently our competition, then *this* is what will show up time and time again in front of us, proving our beliefs to be 'true' and keeping us safe...and also stuck.

We get to create our reality and this is based on the thoughts we think every day.

If we tell ourselves constantly that we won't make a lot of money doing something we love, then BAM, the Genie grants our wish every time.

But same thing goes if we flip it and instead believe that we *can* fully support ourselves and be financially independent and abundant from doing something we love for a living... either way, our wishes come true.

So, I urge you to question the whispers you hear as they get passed down to you from generations before and actively ask yourself if these beliefs are going to *help* you live your best life, get you what you want and enable you to go after your dreams...or not.

If the answer is no, then perhaps it's a good time to start creating a pocketful of beliefs that *do* fulfil all of these things above and then maybe we can start passing *those* ones down to the next generation, so *they* can thrive and enter the world (dance industry included) with a positive attitude, kind demeanour and enough self-belief to fill a nation.

Mind Love:

1. Write down all of the whispers that you believe currently/have been told or passed down to you from teachers, parents or peers and put a tick against all the ones that are positive and help you to grow and a cross next to the ones that don't.

2. Get a new piece of paper and rewrite all of the beliefs with a cross next to them, by turning them into positive beliefs that make you feel excited, exhilarated and empowered.

3. Work at installing these new beliefs daily by reminding yourself of them often (write them in the notes on your phone, inside your mini journal in your bag or on post it notes around your home) so they start to seep into your subconscious mind and eventually become a habit.

CHAPTER 6

POSTURE AND PROJECTION

How do you walk down the street when your favourite song is playing in your ear, you've got a killer outfit on and you just got your hair freshly blow dried?

You don't walk right?

You strut.

And you strut good.

From an outsider's perspective, they have *already* made a judgement that you are a confident, happy and bubbly person, just from seeing you pass them by strutting your stuff with a smile on your lovely face.

Now check it.

How do you walk down the street when you don't make it through the final round of the audition you so desperately wanted, your hair's a sweaty mess and you've got that one song *stuck* in your head on repeat that will haunt you forever as being the song that aided your rejection?

You don't walk right?

You mope.

And you mope good.

Again, from an outsider's perspective, having only just passed by you briefly, they have *already* made a judgement that you are perhaps, a little depressed, your self-care has seen better days and you could *really* use a hug, or maybe just some good vibes sent through the air as physical contact might actually anger you more…and they don't want to take that chance.

I'm sure you've experienced this flash of a pan judgement skill when walking down the street seeing your *own* versions of the above right?

So, what this tells us is just *how* important your posture is, because it's projecting all sorts of powerful emotions out onto those around you.

Now, for some reason, I was born with good posture and have never really had to work on it. Which is a total blessing I know.

But, what I *did* spend a long time working on, was hiding it, so I wouldn't stand out quite so much.

This felt awkward and unnatural to me, because my body is just made to stand tall, because I *am* tall and my spine was created that way, but I hid it all anyway.

Now don't get me wrong, I'm not talking Quasimodo style stooping…more of a head hanging down, leaning to be the same height as my peers kind of jam.

Being the *unbearably* shy girl I was at school, I used to actually hide from boys and if they came to talk to me, well, then I'd roll up my jumper sleeve and cover my mouth if I had to reply, shamefully embarrassed by my teeth, my reddening cheeks and the few little spots I had back then.

Why did I feel the need to do this you might be asking?

Simple really.

I didn't feel good enough.

I didn't *want* to stand out, because standing out meant that there was the potential for judgement and cruelty and my little heart just couldn't take it at the time.

And I never thought to create a scenario in my head where standing out could actually be a *great* thing.

So instead, I hid my light for years and years.

Thankfully, I had people around who saw the light inside me *way* before I did and they encouraged, bolstered and supported me unconditionally and one of those people was one of my first dance teachers.

This woman was respected, admired and appreciated by everyone who knew her. She was firm but fair and she believed in me.

I was always half excited to go to class with her and half terrified that she might decide that I was now out of her circle of trust.

But throughout my seven years dancing with that school, I was *in* and she did *everything* she could to help me progress and develop my skills in a firm but fair manner.

Even though I was given solos, private lessons, asked to assist her in classes and had opportunities others never did, I *still* believed I wasn't good enough.

But she believed otherwise.

It's a wonderful thing to have someone believe in you, even when *you* might not.

Back then, things took a *lot* longer to seep into my system, because *I* was mostly blocking them.

But looking back to all the love that dear woman put into me, all the chances she took on me, all the opportunities she gave to me and all the constant belief she implanted year after year in me, I can now see her point!

And how I definitely wouldn't be where I am today if it wasn't for her.

It can be extremely frustrating and unbelievably obvious to an outsider looking in at you to see all of your amazing qualities, quirks and gifts, when you just *can't* seem to see them for yourself and commit to constantly hiding them away.

But when you're in *such* a self-doubting cycle that seems you'll never escape from, it can feel hard to do anything *but* lock yourself in the bathroom and hope nobody notices (sadly, this one is true).

Have you ever heard the phrase "Fake it till you make it"?

Well, this is something that my mum used to say to me *all* the time when I'd go to her feeling especially insecure and anxious.

So, I'd follow her advice, read one of her many, many self-help books and say to myself, right this is the first day of the rest of my life and I'd try faking it for a while.

Maybe like an hour or two.

It was great, until I forgot, or it just felt too icky and false and then I'd be back to square one again, sticking to the walls of a party, praying I could leave soon (also true, but I was like five years old so this one doesn't count as much).

I think it's all well and good trying the 'fake it till you make it' approach if that feels good for you, but for me, it didn't. So, I spent quite a few more years ducking my head and practicing the sideways lean as I hung out with my friends, on their *physical* level.

What's funny, in a very ironic kind of way, is that one of the main things that has been profound in me stepping into my light, is to give myself love.

Yep, it's the whole self-love shindig again.

I wished it hadn't been the answer, because I found it really, really hard to do.

I didn't *want* to be alone with myself and have a bath whilst reading a book-that made me freak *right* out and caused my heart to pound out of my chest.

But I did it anyway.

I didn't *want* to drive somewhere on my own, with only myself for company, worrying that I might get lost, or forget how to drive or start to hyperventilate in standstill traffic.

But I did it anyway. With music blaring and me singing at the top of my lungs (car dancing and all).

I didn't *want* to start journaling, because that felt weird and woo woo and I was afraid of what would come out.

But I did it anyway and it led to me rekindling my love of writing and ultimately to creating this book.

I didn't *want* to trust my own judgements, intuition or opinions because I was so scared of making a mistake.

But I did it anyway and I got really good at it too.

I didn't *want* to stand out in life, for fear of yet *more* rejection, ridicule and judgement.

But I bloody well did it anyway and I started wearing heels that made me even taller than all my friends and boyfriend, just to make a point to myself.

You don't see Supermodels cowering, do you?

Just saying.

We can say a *whole* lot, without ever having to say anything at all.

Our bodies (especially as movement artists) say everything.

Right now, ask yourself:

"How am I viewed by others in day to day life?"

Consider all the verbal *and* non-verbal communication you put forward to the world and imagine seeing yourself from the outside.

Have you been walking tall, eyes bright and singing to yourself as you bob along the street, or have you in fact been engrossed in your phone, blocking everyone out and created a constant furrowed brow etched into your forehead?

Sometimes we think we are being perceived one way, when really, it's a whole different story.

I remember a time when my anxiety was pretty bad and it was also around the same time that I had just started using the internet for my business and what people told me about their perception of me, truly baffled my mind.

Without hesitation or doubt, they thought I was a bubbly, happy-go-lucky gal, who had life sussed basically!

I was completely surprised, because this couldn't have felt *further* from the truth and I realised just *how* much can be left unsaid online and how potentially dangerous this could end up being.

From then on, I did my best to allow myself to be more vulnerable and real and as a result, more people opened up to me too and I began to feel a healing process take place inside.

So, two things you'll do well to remember when you're going about your daily life are a) never judge a book and b) never assume anything.

When you've established how you think you *may* be presenting yourself to the outside world, now ask yourself the following question:

"How do I *want* to be perceived?"

This is where things get really fun, because you can *literally* be whoever you choose to be (with a bit of discipline and commitment of course) so decide how you *want* to feel, then act on those feelings by creating a life that fills you up so you can.

I always resented being tall, especially as a dancer (the fact that Darcey Bussell was *almost* as tall as me gave me a tiny bit of comfort at least) because tall girls go at the back, which was known throughout dance history and it also meant that I couldn't hide. Ever.

Even *at* the back.

I always checked with my friends what choice of shoe they'd be wearing on a night out, so as to not tower over them and stick out like a sore thumb.

I even remember almost turning back home from a date, because the guy walking into the bar (which incidentally is not the beginnings of a joke) was a *lot* shorter than me *and* tonight I had decided to wear heels.

But when it came to asking myself this question years later, after a lot of soul searching, I concluded that what I really, truly wanted was to be seen.

I *wanted* people to notice me and I'd decided that I was going to own my one, precious body with all of my might-no exceptions.

I now see my good posture and height as the gifts they were intended to be, enabling me to help old ladies reach things from high shelves (literally, happens all the time) stand out in a crowd if I get separated from my family and always be able to clearly see the stage at the Theatre, even if I'm sitting in the stalls.

Oh and of course allowing me to step into my spotlight and be truly seen by the world too.

Body Love:

1. Check yourself every day-what are you putting out into the world? Are you hiding or shining? If you passed yourself on the street, what would you think?

2. Decide how you want the world to see you and then go to town on doing the work on yourself-pour that self-love in and do not stop, ever!

3. Ask around-ask anyone that will listen long enough if they will tell you how they perceive you. Grab a pen and paper because you're going to want to take notes!

CHAPTER 7

DISCONNECT TO RECONNECT

In today's society, if you're not online, you're basically a caveman.

That's the sad truth of the highly technological world we now live in.

However, I *will* give credit where credit is due to the online world because it definitely has its good points; like connecting people from all over the world, allowing you to work from wherever, giving you a space to share your thoughts, talents, business and creatively express yourself in whatever way you feel called and inspired to do.

But as with anything, there's always another side to the story and if you're not using it in the *right* way, the online world has a tendency of swallowing you up whole and then spitting you out again with loads of extra baggage which you now have to carry.

And just *what* is this baggage you may be asking?

Well, you may end up carrying a whole load more comparison in your canvas bag, a rucksack full of not feeling good enough, a handbag filled with envy and a purse full of wasted time.

Now, as I said, the online world *definitely* has its place, but I also remember a time not so long ago when this life didn't exist to the extent it does today and when people actually met face to face, had real conversations and didn't experience this hugely overwhelming feeling of having to record every single inch of their personal and professional life, in the fear that if they didn't post about it, they'd somehow become invisible, or even worse...lose a few followers.

I jest, but I actually held all of these beliefs and carried these heavy bags on my shoulders for many years too.

When I was at dance college, Facebook only turned up towards the end of my first year and when it did arrive, I had absolutely no idea what to do with it.

My friend introduced me to it and I thought it looked like a fun way to connect with some of my old friends from up North and got *so* excited when I found them on there and we became 'friends'. Even though I never actually spoke to a single one of them on the app, ever.

So, a few years went by and I started to get used to the whole Facebook thing. I posted about my holidays and some family events, I checked out other people's pages to keep up to date with what they were doing and when I went to New York City to train at Broadway Dance Center, I made an album with seven hundred and seventy photos in there from my six-month *epic* adventure.

When I went to Thailand with my friend one summer, something we both realised whilst we were away, was that actually, *nothing* was really happening on Facebook from everyone back home. There were some statuses about cats, someone had posted a funny picture of themselves and nothing much after that.

We were in this amazing, tropical place having the time of our lives and back home, life was just normal, as it always was. It seemed almost surreal and strangely shocking at how (before this obvious realisation) we had both been sucked into this normal routine of sharing (or just consuming) our own or other's daily lives without the consideration of *why* we were even doing it.

Back then, I posted on Facebook because I was so excited I could share my adventures with my friends and family in one place, that meant I didn't have to send about fifty different emails or texts to each person with a daily update.

I was 'living my best life' in New York and Thailand as I believe the popular hashtag states and I *really* was. I was present and loving every minute.

But fast forward to when Instagram came about and the pressure was *really* on then.

When I'd posted on Facebook before, my pictures had smudges, they were mid laughter with sometimes a finger over the corner. But now, this Instagram thing had filters and everyone's lives just upgraded from Docu style to super HD film filter and I felt myself sink into this online world of comparison, envy and not feeling good enough.

The funny thing is, I *knew* what I was seeing wasn't real life-but merely a highlight reel presented to the world to show the 'best bits' or 'most motivational, positive posts' and that there was a whole other life *behind* those pictures, some which I knew for a *fact* were not as great as they were portrayed online.

But I found myself doing it too. Stressing each day to find something motivational or visually pleasing to post, with a caption that would blow people away and inspire them to live *their* best life. But behind my highlight reel, I was struggling. I was still suffering with anxiety, low moods, feeling lost, alone and isolated, not properly taking care of myself and feeding off the likes and comments I received to estimate how much worth I held for myself.

Not a great way to live.

But this carried on for years and even though at times my life was crashing down around me, I kept my spirits high for the gram.

The pressure to be positive, excited and just have it together ALL. THE. TIME was exhausting and wearing me down. It wasn't until I *finally* let the true reality sink in and realised that this social media life, was in fact *not* real life, that it *wouldn't* give me the love I really needed, that I *couldn't* get the connection I wanted from it and that it would *never* make me happy, that I started to see it in a whole, new way.

The pressure I was feeling was really coming from *me*, no one else.

The stress of having to post every day was coming from *me*, no one else.

The comparison and envy of other people's lives was coming from *me*, no one else.

I had been using social media as a bolster, to grab self-esteem and self-worth where I could, to use it for all the wrong reasons and unsurprisingly, it never filled me up in the way that I hoped and wanted so badly.

I used to think if I got more likes or followers that would mean I was worthy, it would mean I was a *somebody*, successful or special even. I used to believe that if I could *just* get to 10k, *then* everything would be good and I'd be happy.

But I had got it all so back to front.

I was looking for validation, connection and love from everywhere except myself. So, no wonder those moments of "Yay, I got another ten followers" would only be fleeting, because I hadn't filled myself up *first* and when I consequently lost fifteen followers a few days later, I felt down in the dumps because of that fact.

I hadn't become my own best friend and I hadn't learned that my worth came from *my* own approval, not others.

Social media is a funny old thing, because it really does have the potential to boost a business with its reach, or to make new contacts for networking with, or to create support groups or new friendships that last a lifetime, but when used for the wrong reasons (like looking for validation, love, fulfilment and putting other people in control of your happiness) it can be very, very destructive.

I'm going to assume you use social media, because, well most people do. But, I'm also going to hazard a guess that sometimes you feel the way I did too?

It's hard not to, unless you've done 'the work' on yourself to see social media for what it really is-a platform for creative expression and not a place you go to for love.

So, humour me for a minute.

Let's say you have an amazing dance photoshoot done and you want to share one of your pictures on social media. You post the picture, then the filters come up and suddenly, the colours don't look *quite* as good as if you chose *Mayfair* or *Valencia* on Instagram and you panic that the already edited picture, is perhaps not *quite* as 'perfect' as you first thought.

You choose a filter and carefully create your hashtags, then you click to post and...nothing happens. You check back in five minutes time and *still* no likes or comments. You begin to feel this uneasy feeling in your chest, your heart races and you feel, you feel...unworthy.

Then you check back in thirty minutes time and "Woah, almost one hundred likes" and your self-worth goes through the roof like you're playing King of the Hammer at the arcade.

So, feeling great, you scroll through your news feed and wait, there's a picture of another dancer doing the same pose, but *this* one has one thousand likes and hundreds of comments. So once again, your self-worth immediately plummets and now you feel *even* worse than you did before.

This scenario *was* me! I don't know about you, but I was *so* consumed with what other people thought about me at this time, that something as trivial as a few likes could literally make or break me for an entire day, if not longer.

Which is total madness of course.

You see, when you put your self-worth *outside* of yourself and into the hands of other people, you'll never, ever in a million years, forever and ever amen, feel worthy.

Why?

Because the only person whose opinion, belief and love that *really, truly* matters at the end of each and every day, is yours.

It sounds so simple and kind of boring, because we *all* naturally want to be liked and loved by others, but unfortunately, they can *never* do this for us in the way that we most want them to. That, is up to us.

Let's imagine another scenario now.

You're just back from an amazing dance photoshoot where you felt utterly confident and high on life all day long as you smiled and posed and laughed with your photographer and you now want to share a picture of your fun day on socials.

You get home and you're feeling a little hungry, so your first thought is to make yourself a lovely meal, then you take a nice, long bath and read a book. You're still feeling great and high on life, so you get out your phone, click a picture from the shoot, press post and close down your phone as you get ready for bed, feeling fulfilled and totally content.

The same scenario, but two *very* different outcomes and attitudes.

Here, we see you feeling great consistently because you're listening to what you *need*, you're filling yourself up first and *not* relying on anyone else's opinions, likes, comments or follows to feed your self-esteem or worth.

THIS is what we're aiming for in life. We have to love ourselves so radically that we become the *only* ones whose love we really *need* and count on daily to be happy.

This may sound weird at first, but it actually helps you to love others *way* more than you ever thought possible and makes it much easier for others to love you too.

When we give to ourselves what we need first, whether that be connection, approval, worthiness, belief or love, *we* become the leading character of our own lives and nothing and no one can *ever* disrupt our peace of mind.

You see, when we give ourselves *everything* we need, we no longer put all of that 'stuff' onto others to do it for us (where we simply have *no* control, because as we all know, we cannot control other people) therefore alleviating stress, anxiety and the constant *need* for others to come and save us.

In consequence of being our own saviours, we are then full of everything we will ever need, which means we can then give so much *more* to those around us, without ever *needing* anything back in return.

Of course, it's the best feeling to receive love and be *in* love (which incidentally only happens when *we* are in love with ourselves first) but *without* doing this for ourselves first, we are just relying on other people to fill us up and they can never do that. I mean, pressure!

So, when it comes to social media...use it wisely, know *why* you're using it, understand *what* you're trying to get from it every time you go online and consciously be *aware* of your own needs and *how* you're going to fill them up, without relying on these social platforms to do that for you.

I'm in no way against social media, but I now understand *how* I want to use it and most importantly, *why*.

I no longer seek love and approval from my social platforms, because I make it a daily priority to listen to what I need and ultimately give that to myself first.

I no longer need other people (who remember, most of the time are strangers) on Instagram to make me feel worthy, because, you guessed it, I know my own worth.

I use social media to spread my message and share my passions, so I can hopefully be of help to others in the process.

I use social media to share fun and exciting things when *I* feel compelled to, without the stress of having to post them to get likes or validation.

I use social media as another way of showing my creativity and expression, because I *enjoy* doing that, with no *need* of wanting approval from others.

I use social media as the sauce on top of my cherry on top of my icing on top of my cake, as I live my life in the *real* world and choose to be fully present there, whilst sharing snippets of things that are helpful, useful or fun because *I* choose to.

When we pour love into ourselves and make time for self-care, we begin to reconnect with our soul and our purpose for this life becomes clearer.

Taking time to disconnect from the online world gives us a similar feeling, as we are reminded to live in the moment and tune into how we're feeling and what we need, which always results in us being the best version of ourselves now and for the future.

Soul Love:

1. Life is short and we can miss a lot by wasting time scrolling, comparing and stressing over social media, so try for the next month to switch off for at least one day a week and notice how you feel. This may sound like a *massive* ask, but remember that no one is putting the pressure on you, except yourself. If you go out for a smoothie and don't share it on your Instagram stories, it really doesn't matter. Go and enjoy that smoothie and look up from your phone whilst you're sipping it.

2. When you *do* go on social media, take note of *how* you feel before, during and after. If certain negative feelings are coming up, then ask yourself *why*? You will learn a *whole* lot about what you're searching for in life, when you search for things on social media.

3. Make a cull. Yep, that's right! Stop following people, companies, events, even cafes that aren't in alignment with your values or that create feelings of tension, stress or envy. Just stop following them right now, as of this moment and be strong enough to never check back. Your feed is feeding you, so be very careful with what you allow inside your mind.

4. Find a new hobby! It can feel very strange to disconnect from social media at first and you'll wonder just how you filled your time before Facebook, Twitter, YouTube and Instagram came into being. But this is a perfect time to start a new hobby and disconnect so you can reconnect to what you *really* want and need.

Learn the guitar, start singing lessons, write poems or make jewellery-it can literally be anything that takes your fancy and gets you 'in the zone'. You'll be very surprised at how much progress you can make when you're not wasting time scrolling all day long!

5. Use social media for YOU. Remember, this is *your* account and it's up to *you* how you use it, who you follow, what you post and when. Think about how you want to *feel*, question why you want to use it (what is it giving *you* in return) and then choose whether this is going to satisfy your needs, or whether you can find that sense of worth, love and connection from doing something else in that moment.

CHAPTER 8

MINDSET MUSCLE TRAINING

I didn't hear the term 'mindset' until my mid-twenties. I mean, I probably heard it floating around before seeing as my mum is a Mental Health Practitioner and would talk about this kind of stuff all the time.

But, I never really *heard* it until then, you know?

Before my personal development days began, I thought that I was simply a player in the game of life, with someone else casting the die and me just accepting whatever roll was thrown.

I never really realised or appreciated that *I* was actually the one in charge of *playing* the game and directing my player avatar in whatever direction I chose.

Learning about how powerful my mindset was didn't happen overnight and it *certainly* didn't all click into place at the swish of a wand like I hoped it would.

No, this took years. Years of learning, years of educating myself and years of implementing, getting it wrong, then making progress, only to forget and start again.

I remember in the early days, I'd read or hear something profound, tell my family and friends with such delight and glee and say to myself that everything was about to change and then…nothing!

I was missing the vital piece of the puzzle.

Action.

You can listen to every podcast, read every book, attend every seminar and take part in every course, but if you don't then *act* on what you've learned, you'll stay in the same place forever.

This is what I did. For what *felt* like forever.

And then I wondered why I was *still* struggling, why I felt *so* low and why things just *weren't* changing for me.

Every morning I'd wake up and think, right, today is the day my life changes. Then I'd wait and...still nothing.

I was waiting for someone else to 'do the work' for me and that was *never* going to happen, no matter how much I hoped, wished and prayed.

We come to Earth having one lifelong job...ourselves.

The way I see it is like a lifelong mission or quest and it's all about getting back to yourself, with lots of twists and turns, ups and downs, bumps in the road and rollercoaster highs and then easier terrain for a while and then a few less bumps and a few less twists and turns.

We never 'get there', because *where* is *there?*

Instead, we learn and grow and develop and change and then repeat the process again and again, hopefully becoming more of who we were always meant to be each time.

But this can only happen when we act every, single day.

And by 'act', I mean train your mind consistently so you can have a strong foundation, then act again and again and again each and every day you wake up with breath flowing through your body.

Our minds should come with a 'caution, extremely powerful' sticker so we're always aware of the potential we have inside us.

We can make ourselves believe anything, really, we can!

Just after graduating from college, I flew to Egypt for a dance job (which lasted approximately five days, due to me flying home after what I now deem to have been as sun poisoning- it's real, my friend will tell you...but that's another story!) and I went alone.

Prior to this, I had never flown on an airplane alone before.

I was convinced that I couldn't do it. I couldn't do it when I was twelve and had the opportunity to visit my sister in France, so *why* could I do it now I was twenty-one?

I remember the enormous weight of anxiety I felt before my leaving day arrived and when I got to the airport and my dad waved goodbye to me, I thought I was literally going to pass out from the exertion of my thudding heart.

All the way through the airport I kept telling myself that I couldn't do it, that I wasn't brave enough or wise enough and so it continued, from the check in desk, to the bag drop, to the waiting lounge to the gate.

And then, all of a sudden, I was at the plane door ready to embark on my journey and I think I almost made a run for it, but there were too many people behind me and I didn't want everyone to know *just* how crazy I was.

So, I stepped on to the plane and the kind lady sitting next to me offered me a mint and that made me feel a tiny bit better because I realised that maybe I wasn't *so* alone in the world after all.

A few hours later I arrived in Hurghada airport where I was going to change to another plane for the last hour to Cairo.

I had managed to go this far, yet I was *still* convinced I couldn't go any further. No, this last leg would *definitely* be my downfall.

So, again, mind whirring away against me, I went through the same thoughts and got to the next plane door and realised that this plane was in fact, a much smaller one that didn't look or feel particularly safe, but what else could I do, so I got on, fretting and worrying the whole way.

After a *very* bumpy ride, we landed and I was still *so* sure that I couldn't do this whole solo travel thing, then I found my driver and made my way to my accommodation.

As you can see I *did* manage by myself and I *did* get to my destination in one piece.

But I made the experience a total worry fest and not enjoyable at all as a result.

I had convinced myself that I couldn't do any of it, WHILST actually doing it at the same time!

We believe whatever we tell ourselves, but the only reason why I was able to go forward and arrive in Egypt (apart from the Pilot actually flying me over there safely) was that I took ACTION even though my mind was filled with worry and fear.

Despite my negative mind, I felt the fear and did it anyway, as Susan Jeffers so brilliantly puts it.

On my (earlier than anticipated) return, I couldn't have been more different in my approach to the whole flying/solo travel situation (even though physically, I felt at death's door, mentally...I was on FIRE!).

I handled everything and more on that return flight home and navigated my way easily and effortlessly, dealing with unprecedented hiccups along the way, all whilst feeling like I'd lost fourteen stone in a day (thanks Peter Kay!).

What had changed then?

For one thing, I wanted to get home to my bed so I could sleep for about ten days and wake up feeling human again.

But another thing that changed, was my mindset.

I still took the same action, but this time, I *knew* I could handle anything because I'd already done it before and my journey home involved much more disruption, with me stumbling up and down the cabin aisle every few minutes to get to the bathroom and various other airport shenanigans that one hopes not to have to deal with, especially when you feel like you might just pass out at any moment.

I'd had a mindset upgrade and even though my circumstances could have been better, I *chose* to make the best of it and took some confidence away with me for acting so cool in spite of it all.

What we *choose* to believe becomes our reality.

If we choose to believe that we are useless, timid and can't do much, guess what we'll experience...those very things.

But if we choose to believe that we are in fact a Rockstar... we become a Rockstar.

Because I was forced into taking action to get to the place I wanted to go, this actually *helped* me make the shift in my mind.

I had no choice but to act and do the things I was scared I couldn't do, even though I continued to believe them on my outward journey.

But by doing them, I proved to myself that I *could* do them again and so the act of acting, enabled me to act again?

You get me?!

After this brief stint in Egypt, I then went on to fly solo all over the world for various jobs and holidays and each time, although I may have felt a little nervous, I *knew* I could do it, because I'd done it before.

When action isn't *completely* necessary or imminent, we can keep ourselves stuck forever believing old limiting thoughts and convincing ourselves that we are *far* better off not acting because we are fine as we are, *without* having to extend our comfort zone.

For example; not pursuing a choreographic dream due to worry that I simply wasn't good enough to create it...

Then waiting *years* convincing myself of this 'fact', until my mindset became strong enough to tell my old limiting beliefs that they were no longer needed...and I went and did it anyway.

And guess what, it was one of the best projects I've ever done and I *know* I could do it all again with ease.

So, let me ask you-are there things that you're putting off for fear that you 'can't do them' or 'won't be good enough'?

Perhaps a mindset upgrade is in order too?

We are *all* way more capable than we think and even when we start to scratch the surface of what we can achieve, we have only just brushed the tip of the iceberg.

The more we push ourselves to do the things we think we cannot do, the more we realise and believe that we actually *can* do them *and* so much more.

We spend far too much time getting in our *own* way and therefore stopping ourselves from being our best selves, all because we fear the unknown and haven't yet plugged in to our upgrade setting.

In my first end of year show at college, we got to perform as a year group in several really fun pieces, one of which was a Jazz number choreographed by our lovely teacher, I'll call him Jazzy Jim.

Now Jazzy Jim's classes were great fun and he was probably the most laid back, chilled dance teacher we had throughout the three years training at college.

So, when it came to rehearsing his piece in the show, we all knew it'd be a fun one.

But when Jazzy Jim chose me to stand front and centre for part of his piece, I almost crumbled right there on the spot.

I remember so vividly, going for our first rehearsal in the scary top floor studio (where we always thought the ghosts resided-our college was a school way back when, which made it all the more freaky) and making sure I was in amongst the crowd when Jazzy Jim was blocking positions, because in my head, I couldn't handle being seen or having any kind of responsibility of 'leading', because I still believed I simply wasn't good enough, even though I was *desperate* to be seen and recognised at the same time.

So, imagine my surprise when I saw his finger pointing straight at me and him calling *my* name to the front by his side.

I honestly thought he'd made a mistake and almost opened my mouth to ask him if he had got me confused with another girl, but was too scared and in shock to speak, so I didn't say anything and instead, my heart once again, began its pounding.

All throughout the rehearsal, I was kind of in a blur, desperately trying to remember every step so I didn't do it wrong, but at the same time not being able to concentrate as my nerves were just *too* much to bear.

It took me a long time to admit that I deserved that place he had given me in the front centre. But when it came to show day, I of course was feeling *extra* nervous, especially as this was the first time my family had seen me dance since I'd been at college.

But when I hit that stage and took my place, I shone. I loved every minute of being seen and his belief in me that I could 'own' this position of front and centre, had *me* finally believing it too.

I felt so proud to be there, to represent my year group in this leading position, to show my family what I had learned and what I could do and to prove to myself that I was, in fact more than capable and definitely good enough.

It was just one short number in a great big show, but to me, it meant.the world and it was one step closer to me becoming more of who I knew I could be.

Although at first, I struggled with my ingrained beliefs of not feeling good enough, through the sheer act of acting, I replaced this with a new belief, that I could do *anything* I set my mind to.

And you can too.

Mind Love:

1. In order to change our limiting beliefs, we must create new, positive beliefs. So that is exactly what you're going to do! Write down five new upgraded, positive beliefs about yourself and read them often.

2. To make these new, positive beliefs a habit, we must practice daily. So just as you brush your teeth every morning and night, make these new beliefs a habit too, by almost boring yourself with how often you repeat them in your head!

3. Act. Despite your fears, act.

CHAPTER 9

MIRRORS, LIPSTICK AND SILVER BEACH SANDALS

Dance is an aesthetically pleasing artform and therefore requires the dancer to adhere to these prerequisites and uphold the highest presentation at all times.

When you perform in a show, you know that you will be expected to cover yourself in stage worthy make up, often slather yourself with fake tan and go through copious amounts of hairspray.

You are ultimately playing a role of some sort and this is just another layer of your costume.

But when this level of face and body maintenance is expected at an audition or even a class, it can feel like a completely different experience, bringing up feelings that question your self-worth and abilities, as you believe you are being judged on mere face value.

I vowed to myself (and frequently told my family) that I would *never* change to fit in with the dance industry's expectations if they compromised my own beliefs.

That meant that I was *not* prepared to attend an audition scantily clad wearing nothing but a bikini top, fake eyelashes and hot pants.

It just didn't feel right to me.

I almost went to the other extreme and would never properly show off my body, feeling like it was crude or demeaning to do so.

I hid behind clothes that didn't accentuate my slim, toned figure and spent hardly any time on hair and make-up, simply just doing the essentials.

So, my message to every audition panel and class was "If you don't want to take me as I am, based solely on my talent, then I don't want to work for you" and so this stubborn parade continued for many, many years.

Because of the Greek blood running through my veins, I could *really* hold my own if I wanted to and no one and I mean *no one*, could persuade me to do something I didn't want to do.

It's a blessing and a curse to be this strong willed (AKA stubborn).

But all I know is that I missed out on countless jobs because of this fear based, judgemental, limiting belief.

I was totally acting out of fear; fear of having to change or conform to someone else's desires, fear of missing out because I wasn't good enough just the way I was and fear of actually being seen and getting the job.

I wanted to get work because my skills and talents had been acknowledged as worthy enough, *not* because I had blonde hair, red lipstick or a deep cleavage on show.

I felt like if I did those things, I'd become *less* of who I was and that if I *did* get the job, it wouldn't have been because I was technically able to, it would have been because I 'looked the part' and for me and all my years of training, that just didn't feel fulfilling enough at the time.

Also, I was *so* desperate back then to be accepted and hear the words "Emily, you *are* good enough just as you are, even if you have a bad hair day, a pimple on your chin or mascara goop in your eyes" or something to that extent.

I was craving validation from everyone, especially the audition panel, to tell me that I didn't have to put on this show, because just as I was, was all that they needed. Rather than doing that for *myself* and having the deep knowing that I *was* good enough to start with.

I never saw these 'added extras' for what they truly were-just 'added extras'!

We all know how putting on a little black dress, a pair of killer heels and your favourite lippy can make you feel, right? You become this unstoppable, confident force and all you've done is just accentuate the *you* that was there all along.

But because of my one-sided view, I had forgotten that the dance industry *is* about the look of something-when you watch a show, you can't close your eyes to appreciate the movement, can you?

Everything about dance is about *seeing* it in front of you to appreciate it, unless you're the person dancing, then it is of course about *feeling* it.

I didn't understand that I could *still* be myself, even if I did slap on some lipstick, wear clothes that showed off my figure and got out my GHDs.

These 'added extras' are just part of the costume. They're for accentuating purposes *only*.

And that meant that there would also still be room for artistic licence to show my *own* creativity in putting my best self forward.

The fact is, the dance world is about the *whole* package. And I'm not just talking about being a triple threat with dancing, singing *and* acting under your belt.

I'm talking about you. *You* are the whole package in yourself and it's your choice whether you put that forward or not.

In just the same way that a business woman puts on her suit, slicks back her hair and grabs her engraved laptop bag; dancers simply reach for their shiny leggings, studded bra top and thick eyeliner.

It's all part of the gig.

After attending an audition for an agency I *desperately* wanted to be part of, I was singled out and told to wait behind because they wanted to talk to me.

The lead guy brought me to one side and told me that there was absolutely nothing wrong with my dancing abilities-quite the opposite actually, but I wouldn't be going through because I needed to work on my personal style.

In my head I was dumbfounded, I mean, they had basically told me that I was *more* than good enough and yet, I *still* wasn't getting on to their books? What?!

He then brought over another girl who was *super* tanned, had slicked back hair into a long ponytail, thick make up, tight low waisted wet look leggings and a leopard bikini top on.

I said hello to the girl, feeling just a *tad* awkward in my sweats and converse boots and turned to face the guy. He kind of just waved his arm up and down in front of her and said "This, *this* is what we're looking for" and I *immediately* felt red hot in the face as I realised how inferior I felt standing next to her.

In my head, I had already decided to give up hope and chosen to focus on the fact that they were just interested in aesthetics, rather than true talent, so I nodded my head and skulked out of the studio trying my best *not* to cry my eyes out.

If I had been smart and *not* acting out of my ego, I would have taken his advice on board, put together some ideas on Pinterest of what I wanted *my* style to look like, gone shopping for a few 'added extras' and practiced working on my self-esteem and confidence.

But instead, I just did the same as before and then auditioned a year later having not changed a thing, because *I* didn't need to change, they did (Ego Ego Ego, Oi Oi Oi!) and consequently didn't get picked again, then moped about even harder…even though I hadn't actually done what they'd *specifically* told me to do to get on their books.

Whoops!

If I'd have dropped my ego for like ten seconds, I would have realised that these 'added extras' were simply helping me to *feel* the part, to step up and step into my spotlight and to ultimately, bring out the best *me* that I had to offer.

And they didn't have to involve a leopard bikini *or* wet look leggings if I didn't want them to either. There was *always* a scenario where I could still be me *and* choose 'added extras' that made *me* feel good and suited *my* personality, but I didn't register this at the time.

Subconsciously I was keeping myself safe, convincing myself that I was standing by my principles, rather than just being scared to really let myself be seen, in case I *did* actually get chosen.

Hiding myself away wasn't *just* saved for my dancing life though. I basically went around every day trying to find ways to diminish my light so others wouldn't see me and I could avoid them perhaps passing judgement or criticism that I was too big for my boots or worse, that I didn't actually *have* a light to shine.

What a waste!

I had a six pack that I would never show, I wouldn't wear bright lipstick because it attracted too much attention, I'd always choose flats so I didn't tower above others or stand out in a crowd and I opted for black clothes A LOT. I felt like black was a safe choice as it kept me hidden and would just proceed to tell people that I felt that black was 'Classy' or 'Sophisticated' so they wouldn't know the real reasons behind my concealment.

I would see other women around me looking beautiful in vibrant clothes, or cool make up and of course, *they* stood out and part of me wished that I was brave enough to do that too, but the other part reminded me that I wasn't confident or good enough to even try, so I consequently didn't bother.

When I first went to college and saw that they used mirrors in almost *every* class, I freaked out and don't think I looked myself in the eye until long after I'd left. It felt wrong to give myself *so* much attention and stare at a person that I just didn't feel connected to. That was an extremely hard hurdle for me to overcome and it definitely didn't happen overnight.

But what was *even* harder than looking at myself, was touching myself (now wait a minute before you think this has turned Rated 18 OK?). After graduating from college, I held the belief that hands and arms were made for moving *outside* and *around* the body in dance, not *on* it.

Looking back, it seems so strange to think that I never wanted to touch my *own* body when moving-I mean, I must have looked like a Barbie doll-arms mid-air, carefully avoiding any skin on skin action!

It all came down to me *not* feeling connected to myself or good enough. It just felt weird to look at myself or put my hands on my body, even if it *was* part of the dance and a way of increasing the expression and emotion I was trying to deliver. And what I *also* didn't realise, was that the reason I couldn't do *any* of this, was because I was *seriously* lacking in self-love.

It took a long time before I felt brave enough to put my hands on my body whilst dancing and *even* longer to actually accept that it was, not only *okay* to do that but that it a) added to the emotion and expression of my movement and b) by touching my body, it would actually *help* me to feel connected to myself.

And giving my reflection the eye, well let's just say that I can appreciate the purpose and the lessons that the bright shiny wall now gives me.

I use mirrors to check and correct my technique, to study my lines and poise and to *constantly* challenge myself to look deeper into myself and remain connected to the person staring back.

At my college graduation, we were given letters about our attire for the day and how we would be heading up on stage to accept our Degrees and Diplomas.

I had *no* clue what to wear and was *so* anxious about standing out if everyone else was just going to be wearing 'normal' clothes, so I decided to wear my long black (of course) pinstripe trousers, a black (argh!) short sleeved shirt and a white belt.

It was a boring combination I can tell you. But at least it felt safe.

I *had* got some heels at least (black obviously) so that was my saving grace.

I didn't know it, but I was about to be tested on this graduation day and it was going to be a humdinger...

My friend had brought her car to college for the day, so a few of us had arranged to go with her to the Theatre for our graduation. But for some reason, we were all running really late and so when I got in the front seat of her car breathless and a little dishevelled, I reached into my bag to change into my heels (as I'd had to do a Peter Kay dad run in my beach sandals all the way to her car) and realised, to my utter horror, that I had only packed one shoe.

One of the most organised people in the world and I'd only packed one heeled shoe for my graduation day.

I *begged* my friend to turn the car around and make a detour past my house so I could run in and grab the other one, but she said there simply wasn't time because we were already cutting it fine as it was.

I sank back in the seat and felt so annoyed and upset with myself.

What was I going to do? I couldn't hobble around in one heeled shoe in front of an auditorium full of parents, peers and teachers!

So, about an hour later, we were all in the changing rooms getting our gowns on and *now* to my utter horror again, *everyone* was in beautiful cocktail dresses and looked absolutely gorgeous.

I felt *totally* devastated and embarrassed. This was one of the *biggest* days of my life and I just looked, well, ordinary.

As we lined up inside the Theatre on the top of the steps, with our parents and teachers all eagerly watching, I felt my cheeks flaring up with embarrassment as we walked down and I went up to accept my Degree and Diploma on stage in front of all my peers and the full audience.

There I was, in *all* black attire, with silver, sparkly beach sandals and no nail varnish, tripping on my extra-long pinstripe trousers as I walked up the stairs stage left, my mortification making me feel numb as I shook hands with the head of our college and tried to smile through it all.

Everyone was *far* too busy to even notice of course; I mean, it was graduation day after all!

But *I* knew and I felt awkward and like I'd *really* been taught a lesson (one I didn't learn for years to come mind you).

In life, we are *all* given special gifts, attributes and talents and it is *our* job to make the most of them, whatever they may be.

Now I'm not saying I should have received my awards wearing a crop top and hooker heels, but I mean, sparkly silver beach sandals?!

It is our responsibility to make the most of ourselves. And by doing this, it in no way diminishes our core values or true self, but instead highlights it even more, enabling us to *really* shine our light for all to see.

We spend *so* much time worrying about what other people think of us, not wanting to take up any space in the world and believing that we're not good enough to shine our light anyway.

But the truth is, there's *no* truth in it.

You were put here for a reason.

You were given gifts that need to be shared with the world.

And *you* were born to shine.

On the day I left home for my first year at college, my wonderful parents dropped me off at my new digs and handed me a little book.

It was a notebook that they had filled with beautiful, inspirational quotes and sayings, which of course made me cry and then immediately want to return to the nest as soon as I'd read it!

But one quote that really stands out for me now is this:

"Hide not your talents, they for use were made. What's a sundial in the shade?" -Benjamin Franklin

If you're someone who constantly worries about what other people think, just know this:

No one is really thinking about you at all!

When my mum first told me this as a teenager, I felt extremely offended, because I thought how rude it was that people didn't care about others (Doh!).

But you'll come to see (as I definitely did) that we're all just thinking about ourselves-focusing on where we want to go and how we'll get there, worrying about other people (and *they're* just worrying about other people and so on) and so stuck inside our own heads to even have the *space* to concern ourselves with another person and whether their dress is too short or their job is acceptable etc...

Life is short and so is our attention span these days.

So, decide right now to start making the most of yourself, letting go of what other people think of you and sharing your *full* self with the world, because the truth is, we *need* you to.

There will *always* be people who don't like your audit outfit, or choice of false eyelashes, or pirouette landir or house or car or whatever...but just know that *you* car change this or *them* and that really, it has absolutely *nothin* to do with you and *everything* to do with them.

Even though they are aiming their comments in your direction, their thoughts are still inside their own head thinking about themselves and worrying (just like we all do) about what other people are thinking about *them*.

Be your best always and just let the haters hate, because it'll give them something to do with their time and energy whilst they're still figuring out their own *stuff* and we *all* need an occupation, right?

It is time, my dear friend, for you to step into your spotlight.

And about time too.

Body Love:

1. In every opportunity you have to do so, make the most of yourself and own it.

2. Remember that you are *more* than good enough just as you are and that there's nothing wrong with adding a few extras to accentuate your gifts.

3. Stand naked in front of the mirror and just look at yourself. Appreciate everything about yourself, remark on all the amazing bits about your body and give praise to them. Then make it a game to find and wear clothes, accessories, footwear and make up that help you to feel like a million dollars and more.

4. Own it.

CHAPTER 10

DO YOU WANNA BE IN MY GANG?

I remember the first time I went to an audition on my own. My heart was racing double time and I almost convinced myself that I shouldn't go in. You know the drill by now, my mind was doing its usual "You won't get it anyway", "Everyone else will be better than you" blah blah, bloody blah.

But I went anyway, despite the anxiety coursing through my body (you'd think I was putting myself through torture not my favourite pastime!).

As I approached the studio doors, scared that someone would hear the almighty thudding coming from my heart, I entered and made my way over to the reception desk.

Feeling *very* vulnerable and anxious already, I was literally on the brink of crying my eyes out should anyone pass an unfair comment my way (great idea to attend an audition then right?).

I'll never forget the palpable tension, stares and what *I* perceived as ice cold unfriendliness, as I entered the changing room that morning to get myself ready.

I felt like it was me against *every* other girl in there and even though I tried to smile through my anxious state, *no one* returned it back to me.

At the time, I was as I said, extremely vulnerable and a situation like that would dictate my mood and focus for the rest of the audition day (and then some).

I felt like I had done something *wrong* to those other girls; like I had angered them by showing up, or annoyed them because I wasn't worthy of being there (I know, I know).

But at the time, it all felt *very* real and probably why I used to let people go ahead of me in the audition room and encourage *them* being seen by the panel, rather than myself.

Basically, I didn't feel good enough to be there.

I so *desperately* wanted to feel accepted and like I belonged, but all I was greeted with was animosity and exclusion.

Especially when another girl would come into the *same* changing room and immediately be greeted by another girl with shrieks and hugs and smiles.

I took it all *very* personally.

And when I got cut from the audition, well, that was already set in the cards because I *knew* I wasn't as good as everyone else there.

Have *you* ever felt like this?

What amazes me now is how insular I was.

How much I cared about what other people thought of me.

How I *let* other people dictate my state of being.

And how I *never* thought for a moment, that it wasn't even about me at all!

I was so intent on being accepted by my peers in the industry, because if *they* accepted me, well, then maybe that meant I *was* good enough after all.

I put *so* much pressure on everyone else to make me feel worthy, when what I really needed to be doing, was focusing on doing that for myself.

The girls in the changing room that day and every other day I auditioned or took a class weren't concerned with *me*...they were thinking about themselves.

They had their *own* anxieties and worries to deal with and everything revolved around *their* world and *not* mine as I had always thought.

When someone they knew entered that room, their heart was able to relax a little and it gave them some tiny relief to know that *they* were not alone in this world either.

Remember, at the end of the day, we all want the same things; connection, acceptance and love.

A few years later feeling a little bit wiser and a *lot*, lot braver, I felt a stirring in my soul and decided to move to the *"concrete jungle where dreams are made of"* ...New York City.

I had been accepted on to an International Student Visa Program at Broadway Dance Center that would last three months (which turned into six, because I just simply couldn't tear myself away).

On my solo flight over to New York, I was feeling 50% petrified and 50% "THIS IS THE BEST MOMENT OF MY ENTIRE LIFE" as I sank back into my seat ready for my seven-hour movie marathon.

Something happened to me during those six months and it happened really quickly (after the initial shock of being in another country alone not knowing anyone had worn off of course).

I felt transformed.

Everything was bigger, brighter and just *better* over there.

I could be *whoever* I wanted and had the freedom to explore my passion in the greatest place on Earth (go on, disagree with me, I dare you!) and I was happy all the way through to my core.

I felt confident and sassy, I walked a little taller (with a bit of a hip sashay going on too) and I properly *believed* in myself for what felt like the first time in my life.

THIS made *all* the difference to the quality of my life.

I could feel it. I felt like I was capable of *anything*.

And my experience of changing rooms in New York was a *whole* different story.

I remember feeling the same nerves and familiar heart thudding on my first day at Broadway Dance Center as I entered the building, but that quickly evaporated as I was greeted with smiles and cheerful hellos from the reception desk.

Okay, so far so good.

Then upon entering the dreaded changing rooms, I was *again* greeted with smiles, a few hellos and small chit chat as I placed my bag down to change.

Okay, now this was freaky.

I went into my class, not knowing the rules for this new environment and was yet again greeted with smiles and friendly faces surrounding me.

Something wonderful was happening!

My passion for dance was returning and I felt confident and free.

I felt like I had missed out on this whole other side of the dance world that was the personification of fun and happiness.

I was in my element and my self-worth was sky high.

The most wonderful thing about my whole experience there, was the people I met and the friends I made.

Being on the International Student Visa Program, I met people from *all* over the world and I *mean* all over; from Sweden to South Africa, from Germany to Guatemala, from Uruguay to USA, from Australia to Argentina, from Italy to India and from Japan to…just down the M25 from me.

Everyone I met was wonderful.

There was no bitchiness, no competing, no rudeness or selfishness, just a great big family full of love.

I had found my tribe and I definitely wanted to be in their gang.

But what was the difference then?

Why was there *such* a stark contrast between my experience in the UK and the one I was having in NYC?

Me.

That was the difference.

In the UK, I was a shell. Surviving on whatever compliments, validation and recognition I could get, because I didn't believe in myself or my abilities and *certainly* never showed myself any love or care at that time.

I had spent years believing certain myths and limiting beliefs about myself *and* the industry and saw these to be true because *that* was my experience (because *that* was in fact, what *I* was projecting out into the world) and therefore they *became* fact and *couldn't* be changed in my eyes.

But when I was in a new place, a magical land full of opportunity and freedom, I could be whatever I wanted to be. I could rewrite my beliefs and I could start again with love at the forefront.

Love for dancing.

Love for my peers.

And love for myself.

I was no longer a shell, I had blossomed into the best version of me and all I wanted to do was live that every day.

So, guess what happened...

All of my experiences reflected this *new* belief and I had an absolute blast the *whole* time I was there.

Now, I'm not suggesting you hop on the next flight to New York (although really, I would never discourage that) so you can experience a mystical transformation the moment *you* set foot on US soil.

No, what I'm merely pointing out, is that when *I* changed, my life changed with it.

For me, moving to New York was the best decision I could have made for myself at that time. It was *exactly* what I needed to push me out of my comfort zone, encourage me to be brave and give me *so* many life lessons that mostly eluded to me just being my best self and enjoying the heck out of life.

You know that feeling you get after a really relaxing holiday, or a long soak in the tub, or a walk through nature, or when Spring finally arrives?

That feeling of hope, inspiration and excitement.

Ideas start flowing, you feel connected to the world and ready to take on life...

That's what my time in New York gave me.

After being *so* unhappy and low for such a long time, I was given a *massive* wake-up call to shock me back to life again!

Learning that *I* was actually the one in the driver's seat, gave me so much confidence and helped me to heal from the inside.

I had been searching for years for acceptance and approval from my peers and those around me, when really, I could have saved myself the struggle, if I'd only looked in the mirror a bit more often and checked *there* for the answers.

When I found my tribe in New York City, I really found myself.

Everything I had been looking for, was just buried deep inside me waiting to burst out.

We search for connection at every turn, trying to find it in other people and outside experiences and this may work for a short while, yes.

But, unless we are connected to the one person who is going to see life through with us until the sweet end, we can't feel truly alive or happy.

This is why it's so important to spend time *on* yourself and *with* yourself. To nurture your tribe of 'me, myself and I' and do everything you can, to create inner happiness, *without* the distraction of other people or outside circumstances and events.

The reason I was *so* consistently happy in New York, was because I felt happy in *myself* first.

But to do this, to *really* be happy and the best version of you consistently, takes courage, persistence and as my sister so wisely says, "constant, wilful discipline" every, single day to create and maintain a garden of peace inside you.

New York City is for me, the greatest place in the world.

And no wonder really, it was the place of my rebirth and transformation and holds *so* many wonderful memories, places and people.

It's where I feel most at home and connected to myself *and* something bigger.

But I also know, that this wonderful feeling of belonging and contentment can be found inside me at *any* time, *wherever* I am in the world; whether that's on a busy tube in London, feeding Kangaroos in Australia, on a beach in Bali, or sitting with my laptop looking out at the mountains in Wales as I write this chapter.

And whilst the above paragraph is true, because we will always be responsible for choosing our emotions and how we respond to *everything* in life, I must also state that certain environments and places *can* instil an extra sense of passion, motivation and excitement that helps you to feel even *more* like your best self, as New York did and *still* does for me.

You *too* can find yourself...and you don't even have to board a plane to do it.

Before you try looking out there, take a moment to look inside instead.

The place you belong, your tribe or your gang, are with you wherever you go, because they're all in *you*.

YOU are where you belong.

...but if you *also* find that you belong in New York City, then be sure to look me up, because I'm always available for trips to the Big Apple!

Soul Love:

1. Get a piece of paper and a pen and think about how you act in different scenarios and places... are you consistent? Or are you different? Do you feel more alive in certain places and with certain people? Do you feel unenthused in others? Write out as much as you can.

2. Next, read everything back that you wrote down and try to connect the dots; ask yourself *why* you feel the way you do and see if you can pinpoint recurrent themes as to why this might be. Keep this light and allow time and space for thoughts to come to you, if they don't at first.

3. In the situations where perhaps you *don't* feel like your best self, could you perform a little mindset upgrade and create some new beliefs that would allow you to step up? Take each one and do your best to think "If I were my best self, how would I *be* in this situation?" and then go out and try it!

CHAPTER 11

THERE'S ROOM FOR EVERYONE IN THE CHANGING ROOM

I'm just going to go right ahead and say it.

I used to be *super* jealous of other people's success and resent the fact that *they* had achieved all of this cool stuff and felt it was *so* unfair that I hadn't achieved exactly the same things, without really looking at my own life to see all the cool stuff I'd already done.

Relate much?

Not a great colour on me, I'll admit it.

But when you're ruled by your emotions (and ego) this is a *totally* common response to have.

I used to think that other people getting cool parts in the show, getting to the next round in the audition, having amazing photoshoots or getting the dream job meant that somehow, *I* wasn't good enough to do all of these things too.

So, as a 'go-to' reaction I always went with resentment, jealousy, feeling put out, thinking "why them, not me, it's so unfair" instead of celebrating my peer's successes like they were my own and realising that there *is* in fact, more than enough good stuff to go around and that I needed to make a few mindset shifts pronto, if I was *ever* going to get away from this lack mentality.

I was under the impression that if my friend got a starring role in the end of year show, *that* somehow meant that I was useless, redundant, or to say it bluntly…a failure.

I thought that *I* deserved these successes just as much as anyone else, but never got those things because 'life was just so unfair'.

Oh, woe is me...

On the outside I clapped and cheered for the other person who had what I desperately wanted, but on the inside, I was dying, feeling like I would never achieve my goals or experience the same success that *they* had.

As I said, not a great colour on me.

Instead of always choosing the fear and lack mindset (that's super easy to do by the way, especially when it's something you've always done...I mean, err hello established habit that's not actually serving me) which was keeping me depressed, aiding my ever-fading low confidence and self-esteem, I could have gone down the other route and chosen love.

In life, we're either choosing love or fear. Maybe this is the first time you've heard that?

Or maybe it's the hundredth.

This took me a *long* time to understand and change, because for so much of my life, I chose fear.

And even though this choice never served me, I continued to do it, because under the surface I was getting benefits that my conscious mind wasn't aware of, but my subconscious mind wanted to keep getting (to keep me safe I might add).

Let me break it down a little more.

By choosing fear/lack/negativity, I was keeping myself stuck and therefore I didn't have to change anything.

Any of this sound familiar?

So, by not changing anything (even though I was desperately unhappy), I was safe.

Because change means that things will be different and different = scary/not safe/danger to the subconscious mind.

You know when there's something you really want to do, but as soon as the excitement fades, the fear kicks in and somehow, you've managed to talk yourself out of doing said thing by conjuring up all sorts of excuses as to why you can't/no longer want to/the timing isn't right etc...

Well, that's your subconscious keeping you safe and let's face it, coddled in cotton wool so you never spread your wings and see what life has to offer you.

And the subconscious mind is only doing its best to protect you I might add, so let's not be all judgemental and start berating it, because it just doesn't *know* any better!

Let's instead, start to pay a bit more attention to it and begin to nurture it, so that when we *do* have to react or decide, we choose the love option *more* than the fear.

I remember a time, back in dance college when one of my best friends got a coveted role in the end of year show...and I didn't. It was the role I wanted so badly, the role I felt I'd been working so hard to achieve and when it was given to my best friend, I felt crushed.

But on the outside, I smiled and congratulated her and tried my best to hide my utter devastation.

She was beautiful in the role and really gave it her all, but I still felt a hurtful sting inside my heart every time I looked back on the event for years after.

This caused me much sadness and pain, because I'd chosen to act out of fear, not love.

I chose to see my friend's success as *my* downfall.

I chose to see my friend's success as *my* failure.

I chose to see my friend's success as me *still* not being good enough.

When in fact, if I had acted out of love, I would have seen a few different things instead.

I would have seen that my friend's success, was a guiding light showing me *and* everyone else what was possible.

I would have seen that my friend's success, allowed me to see the things I truly wanted from life, where maybe before I had felt clouded by my goals.

I would have seen that my friend's success, didn't abolish my own in any way and that by not getting this dream role, I was being redirected to something more suited, for *me*.

And I would have seen that this was an opportunity for me to practice giving *love* and supporting my best friend as she courageously stepped out of her *own* comfort zone.

It might feel hard to see those you love around you getting the things that *you* want for yourself, but it's actually only hard when we decide to choose fear over love.

We seem to, as humans, focus on the *one thing* that's not going well/we don't yet have/is a problem in our lives, instead of putting *all* of that energy into loving the pants off everything that *is* amazing, golden and wonderful.

When I *chose* to focus on the negative and let fear consume me, I missed out on all the good stuff that *was* actually happening for me at that time.

I was surrounded by a group of *super* supportive, trustworthy friends who loved me, I had a family that was always there for me no matter what, I was healthy and able to do what I loved every day, I had regular opportunities to perform, teach and dance, I was able to be independent and I had food, water and a lovely roof over my head too.

The reason I reacted *so* strongly to my friend's success, was that at that time, I had very little self-confidence, self-esteem, self-worth and self-belief. I expected to *not* do well, because I wasn't as good as everyone else (or so my mind told me again and again).

So therefore, I was relying on outside forces and circumstances to change how I felt about myself and give me bucket loads of self-confidence, self-esteem, self-worth and self-belief, because *other people* believed in me and not because *I* believed in me.

When reading this, it may seem obvious to you that this way of living my life was extremely back to front and unhelpful. But at the time, I *truly* believed that for me to have a life I loved and be the best possible version of myself, I needed *other people* to get me there.

Talk about not taking responsibility for myself!

Perhaps you're now thinking back to a time when you may have had a back to front mentality too?

Not *only* was I choosing fear back then, I was also *heavily* relying on outside circumstances to make me happy.

The reason I let myself be crippled by fear and rejection from my best friend's success, was because of the following belief:

I believed that by getting that role in the show, I would be happy, successful and *finally* think that I was good enough.

So, by *not* getting this role (and pinning *everything* on it) I felt like these feelings had passed me by and I would never be happy, successful or good enough.

Of course, at the time I didn't realise any of this.

At the time I was still stuck in the "Why her, not me" phase (which is *so* not pretty by the way, just in case you were thinking of adopting that reaction next time things don't go the way you want).

I was doing life in a very back to front way.

When you put expectations outside yourself to make you feel a certain way, you will *forever* be disappointed and live life in a fear-based state.

There was never a scenario in my mind that involved *all* my friends and I getting equal successes in our lives-it was always an either/or situation.

Either *I'll* get the role or *she* will.

Either *I'll* perform on stage or *she* will.

Either *I'll* get the contract or *she* will.

But how about a life where *everyone* comes out on top.

Where we're *all* able to celebrate each other's successes as if they were our own.

Where we don't compete with each other, but instead cheer for each other.

Where we *each* get what we want and are happy for not only our own successes, but truly, honestly, deeply happy for our friend's too.

It's no guesses which option is going to give you everything you want and which one will leave you feeling depleted, fearful and depressed, right?

In the world today, it can feel commonplace to think you're competing against your friends and peers.

But what if we choose to come from a place of love and know that there is *more* than enough for everyone to succeed and achieve their wildest dreams…which, by the way doesn't mean you stand back and wait for everything you want to come to you (without you actually having to do anything)…it means taking action but from a place of love *not* fear, doing your best and whatever the outcome, knowing that what is meant for your highest good will always prevail.

The Universe/God/Zeus, is not trying to mess with you on purpose (even though sometimes it may feel *exactly* like that), but instead guiding you towards your truest path in life, which may turn out to be something you've been resisting or not even been aware of.

So, stay open, know that there's room for *everyone* and all their pets in the changing room and celebrate everything, because *"a little party never killed nobody"* right?

Mind Love:

1. Take out a pen and paper, or grab your journal and write down anything that came up for you regarding other people's successes whilst reading this chapter. Be honest in your feelings and if you do discover some negativity/fear flowing out on to the page, then stop for a second and think about why these emotions are rearing their heads? How's your self-belief doing right now? Where's your self-love game at? How about your self-worth…what is it really worth to *you*?

2. When we take a step back from the pain, we can see more clearly and deal with the facts in a logical way. Remember, someone else's success does not diminish your own, nor does it mean you are unworthy, nor does it mean that there isn't anything left now for you… have a quiet, soft word with yourself and choose love.

3. When you've chosen love, then give a whole load of it to yourself in the form of quiet meditation time where you can reconnect to yourself, listen to affirmations, write out your goals and what truly lights you up and keep affirming your worth every single day by becoming your own best friend-talk to yourself, cheer yourself on, give yourself praise and love without needing these things from anyone else first.

CHAPTER 12

IT IS *NOT* PERSONAL

Being a sensitive soul, I always took *everything* and I mean everything to heart. I felt like anything negative that was said to me was a personal attack and have probably accrued *years* of crying into my hands, sniffling and mumbling about how life was just *so* unfair and people were mean.

I mean what a waste of good eyeliner right?

Having low self-confidence and self-esteem, people's comments and criticisms affected me greatly, because *all* I wanted was to do the right thing, say the right thing and be a good girl, so I would be praised, complimented and validated.

This unrealistic expectation was what I hung *all* my hopes on to feel good each and every day of my life.

Man, that was exhausting. I mean, even just writing about it has me in need of a little lie down and a nice cold flannel on my forehead.

Anyway, I digress.

This was a *huge* responsibility and expectation I put on every person I ever came into contact with and something I *never* realised I was doing for *literally* a decade.

I mean, I was calculating my self-worth on the positive responses *other people* gave me daily and when I didn't get what I needed, well, let's just say I definitely got the Greek temperament from my dad...

The trouble with living in this way, although totally naïve and honest in its own right, is that it puts *other* people in control of your happiness and not the one person who actually *can* control it (it's you by the way, just in case that wasn't clear yet).

For someone who placed their happiness and worth on to other people and external circumstances, dance college probably *wasn't* the best place for me at the time...but then again, what better way to learn a lesson than by throwing yourself into the fire, staying there for three years and figuring out how to come out the other side reborn, like a beautiful Phoenix.

Ballet was my first love. It was the first class I ever went to. I used to dance around the house pretending I was the next Darcey Bussell and just loved everything about it; the tutus, the tiaras, the elegant lines and beautiful, ethereal technique...everything was stunning and made my heart that little bit lighter.

I also knew just how hard Ballet was, out of every dance style, Ballet involves the most technically advanced movements and positions and requires you to truly test your body in every way possible.

So, to say I was a little apprehensive of my Ballet classes at college, was an understatement.

Never before had perfection to this extent been required of me and I felt a *huge* amount of pressure to fulfil this requirement, especially as I was put in the top Ballet group and therefore felt I needed to prove myself at *every* available opportunity.

Fortunately, I *loved* my Ballet teacher...at first. And he seemed to have a little soft spot for me too...at first.

He was the most energetic, exuberant, passionate man I think I've ever met and his classes were fast paced, challenging but fun.

At the beginning of my first year at college, I *really* enjoyed his classes. They were the Ballet lessons I looked forward to and felt like I was actually making progress in.

I had also been picked to take part in the Pas De Deux classes taught by him, which were only reserved for a select few and *me* getting picked really gave my confidence a huge boost, but ironically also brought on *even* more anxiety and self-doubt in the process.

I felt *even* more expectation to be seen as 'good enough' and I put a lot of pressure on myself to get things right, *all* of the time.

As I may have mentioned previously in this book, I was a shockingly shy girl, (except on stage ironically) and needed a lot of gentle coaxing to get the 'performer me' to come out in class and day to day life.

So, when my Ballet teacher gave me a compliment, I hung on to that good feeling (and wrote it in my diary to remember too obviously) like I was desperately clinging to my life vest as the ship went down. I was sky high and felt pleased with myself that I had given him what *he* wanted in class.

Then one day, the teacher we all knew and loved changed, as if overnight and his passionate flair was replaced with a constant frustrated furrowed brow and critical comments flying out of his mouth in every class he taught from then on.

I took everything he said to heart. He was someone I had looked up to, respected, admired and loved learning from. But now, now I was scared to go to his classes, I dreaded the inevitable criticism that was coming and I began to lose my enjoyment of Ballet.

When you're a constant worrier and battling with anxiety, depression and self-doubt, you feel like everything in life is about *you*. Even though, it is most definitely not.

This change in his behaviour felt *very* personal and I even felt partly responsible for it, like I should have tried harder or practiced more, *then* he would have been his usual happy self.

His new demeanour continued and I couldn't comprehend it throughout my whole time left at college. I was convinced that it was somehow *my* fault still and made it my responsibility to worry about it, *a lot*.

Now this isn't the only time I've felt like this and it didn't stop with the dance world. I felt responsible for the problems of my family/boyfriend/friends/strangers I'd just met and felt a constant heavy weight pressing down on my shoulders with the burdens of carrying other people's 'stuff' thinking that *I* was always to blame for it.

Perhaps you've felt a similar thing in your own life?

Well if you have, I'm about to say something so profound, you might not even see it coming...

It. Is. Not. Personal.

See, I told you, you didn't see it coming right!

Other people are *not* your responsibility, that is because everyone is each in charge of their own 'stuff' which they may or may not decide to bring to the party.

What I didn't realise at the time, was that my Ballet teacher's change of mood had absolutely *nothing* to do with me.

Surprising that. And by thinking that it was, I was actually being quite self-righteous (without knowing that of course) by assuming that I had *that* much power, influence or effect over someone else.

The fact was, he had his own 'stuff' going on and had chosen to deal with it in the way *he* knew how to. Even if that meant not having to deal with it at all *and* being Mr Grumpy Grumps forever more.

But we can *only* react or respond to the level of thinking that we're at. And if we believe that our reactions are out of our control (which they're not by the way) then we will give in to life and consequently live in a way that makes *other* people wrong and in charge of our happiness (which they're not).

Only *we* are in charge of our happiness-because only WE get to choose how we react to everything in life. Choose love, or choose fear. The choice is always ours.

Another time I fell under the spell of thinking that *I* was the problem, was when my two best friends in college decided one day that they were going to use their own internal struggles and 'stuff' and take them out on me, in style I might add.

I found this one even harder to cope with than my Ballet teacher going Hulk if you'll believe that.

I was instantly drawn to this guy and girl; they were *my* people and we had so much fun together. I felt like I'd found my tribe at eighteen and it consisted of the three of us. I really thought we would be the 'friends forever' kind, but sadly it didn't last.

After living with the girl for six months, a room became free in our flat and we thought it'd be absolutely fabulous to ask our other best friend to come and join the house of fun. So, we did. And he got on board. And we had the best couple of months together.

Until we didn't.

At the time, remember I was in the throes of low self-confidence, self-esteem and self-worth and took *everything* as a personal hit to my core and basically was existing on the validation and love I got from other people, not myself.

So, when my two best friends (and now roomies) began leaving me out, hiding in their rooms together, giving me the cold shoulder and generally acting like I'd just spat in their face, punched them in the stomach and run off with their other halves (none of which I did of course, but you get the picture) I started to feel just a *tad* low and sad and like I didn't want to exist anymore.

I spent *so* many nights in my room feeling like I was going crazy, because during college hours they would act in a civil, almost friendly way, but behind closed doors, it was a whole different story and no one seemed to notice, except me.

I remember one night, when I felt especially bad in myself and I called home for some moral support and a much-needed dose of love as I was left home alone, *again*, as the other two had gone out without me and I was greeted with the happy sound of my dad's voice, who had just left the dinner table where my mum, siblings and niece were, to talk to me.

I cried on the phone (which must be like, the worst thing for anyone, let alone a parent to hear-sorry dad!) explaining my situation and how I just wanted to come home. I made many calls like this during my time at college, all the time feeling out of control of my situation and like everything was happening *to* me.

After we hung up and he had tried to console and reassure me, I broke down even more. I cried my little heart out in that cold, empty room that night and that's when I actually considered ending it all.

Once I'd had that thought, at first, I cried some more, because I couldn't believe I was even thinking such a thing, then I *finally* pulled myself together and gave myself a talking to and realised that no matter how bad I felt, I didn't really want to end my own life.

I couldn't do that to the people I loved and I still felt like maybe, *just* maybe, things could eventually get better somehow and there would be a scenario where I was alive because I desperately wanted to *live* instead.

So, I didn't act on that dark thought and instead I sought solitude and peace of mind in another friend (*still* not realising that the person who could bring me peace, was in fact, inside that cold, empty room all along...but don't worry, it's coming!).

I confided in her and she listened to me and every night after I finished college and made my dinner, I'd walk down to her house (to remove myself from the now unbearable atmosphere of my own flat) and read magazines on her bed, or we'd make cookies, or I'd try and work out her laptop with all the Norwegian keys and play on the internet as she tidied her room for the fiftieth time that week.

It was nice. There was no pressure. She was everything I needed at the time and she was there for me when I felt like I couldn't go to anyone else.

In short, she saved me.

I only confided in this friend about what was really going on at first, because I was afraid of what others would think, still somehow loyal to my two roommates who clearly couldn't give a hoot about me *and* I was also still worried that I was possibly making the whole thing up in my head.

I *still* felt like I had done something *so* horribly wrong and unjust to these two people, but couldn't for the life of me work out what the hell it was!

I drove myself crazy trying to think of every conversation, every action, every thought even…and still, nothing.

I made it personal.

I thought that *their* behaviour was all down to me.

I mean, modest much Emily?!

I joke, but at the time, I couldn't see anything further than my nose and honestly, truly believed (again) that *I* was to blame for their actions.

So, I kept myself miserable (contemplating suicide) because I lacked the belief in myself to know that perhaps this was in fact, *their* 'stuff' and actually none of my business, because I *was* a kind, generous, loving human being after all.

As a result of these events, I consequently moved out and found a much nicer place to live with someone who is still one of my best friends in the whole world (thanks Universe!) cemented my friendship with my little Norwegian pal who years later, I ended up travelling the world with and lived and worked with her in Norway and had the time of my life, removed myself from any situations where my old friends were and concentrated on the people in my life who *did* want to be there.

Years later, I was sat on my laptop at home suddenly remembering the whole thing and feeling just as confused and confounded by it all, wondering if I'd ever know *why* it all happened, when a message popped up on my screen from, yep you guessed it-the girl.

To say I thought this was a freaky coincidence was an understatement, but what came next was just pure Universal magic.

The message, in summary, told me how *sorry* she was for treating me the way she did. How she was going through a very tough time back then and didn't know how to handle it all. And how she was wrong to have put me through all that she did.

I think that is the *only* time in my whole life that I have been so stunned that I was literally lost for words.

I couldn't quite believe what I was reading.

So, all this time, I had done *nothing* wrong after all, it *wasn't* my fault in any way *and*…it wasn't personal.

I sank back in my chair and breathed out after what must have been about an hour of holding my breath for shock.

Then I hastily called my parents in to see the message and they too, were in shock at her contact, but of course knew that it had never been personal and most definitely was never *my* responsibility for her behaviour either.

I never heard back from the guy, but this apology from my girlfriend, was enough.

I knew then that a) it was never personal and b) I could now move on.

Bullying happens all over the world in one form or another and this, this was bullying in adult form, at dance college with bells on.

And why did it happen to me?

Because I was an easy target. I *let* it happen and even *encouraged* it with my own lack of self-respect and belief in myself.

Now I'm not making myself wrong for my actions all those years ago, but at the time, I had very limited self-awareness and took *everything* to heart, so imagine if you were the perp...it'd be a dream to torment me, right?!

You'd get exactly the response/boost you needed, because I didn't fight back, or stand my ground or even just not bother myself with you.

Looking back, it's easy to see where you've gone a little *off* and how you could have done it better right? But life is about lessons and this was a *huge* one for me to learn and I'm pleased to say that I learned it alright.

So, don't ever cross me now!

P.S. I've got Greek blood running through my veins too, so yeah, you don't want to get on the wrong side of that.

Something I've come to realise (that I *never* thought I would) is that I'm beyond grateful for every experience I've had so far. That's right, even those dark, dark times that almost pushed me over the edge.

I'm grateful for them all, because without them, I wouldn't be the person I am today. I wouldn't have learned so many life changing lessons. I wouldn't have grown, or taken leaps of faith, or developed rock solid self-belief to know I can do anything in life...and I *definitely* wouldn't have had as much content for this book!

It is in fact, the harder times in life that seem to give us the most growth if we let them. Without my own, I can guarantee I would have stayed in my comfort zone forever and *never* had the courage or belief that I could try a thing or two and know in my heart, that if things didn't work out so well, well I'd be more than okay with *learning* a lesson or two along the way instead.

From every experience that I may have perceived to be 'bad' back then, I actually learned how to be mentally strong, to seek out deep and meaningful relationships, to not be so 'in my head' and self-centred, to enjoy the small things, to *truly* know I have a wonderful support system in my family, partner and friends, to be independent and trust my choices and to know that I can handle *anything* life may bring my way.

When things weren't going according to my plan, much to my *then* annoyance, my ever-supportive parents would *always* say "It's all good experience Emily" as I rolled my eyes and waited for the same lecture to be over.

But what's funny, is that some part of me knew back then that there *would* come a day where I actually believed their wise words and of course, that day eventually did come.

It can be hard to trust that everything will all turn out okay if you're going through the mill-I know because I used to think there'd never be a way out of my *own* struggles.

But from my own experience (which is all anyone can offer a place of advice from) if you can trust yourself enough to know that whatever comes along, you'll handle it, then you'll be much more equipped to enjoy ALL the ups and downs for exactly what they are-good experience!

Soul Love:

1. When we haven't yet learned how to love ourselves first, we can take every comment/criticism to heart, so our first task is to always fill ourselves up with love. How do we do that? By getting really quiet and asking ourselves questions, by journaling and ultimately by taking action on those things that come up. We must fill ourselves up with love from the inside first, in order to handle all that life brings us-both the positive and the negative.

2. Make a list of everything that makes you feel good-perhaps it's music, animals, your favourite film, a bath, running, travelling...it can be whatever lights you up. Then look at this list and make it a priority to start filling your life with these blessings.

3. Now write down all of your amazing qualities as a human and read this often. Fill your mind, body and soul with as much positivity and self-love and care as you can.

CHAPTER 13

THE GAME CHANGER

When you're experiencing anxiety and depression, the last thing you feel like doing is being grateful.

But gratitude is the game changer.

When things were really on a downward slide in my second year (right before I broke my toe, but just in the middle of my roommate wars) my mum came to visit me for a few days on her own.

I was *so* glad of her company and felt devastated when she had to leave so soon.

Whilst she was with me, I still went to all of my classes in the day and then we'd just hang out at night in my room talking or watching DVDs, trying to keep out of the way of my two roommates and me safely cocooned in her loving, supportive arms.

But on one of the afternoons, I decided I'd have enough time to go home quickly and see my mum before my final class of the day, so I made my way back to my flat as quickly as I could, eager to get another boost of love and support in me before going back to my lesson.

When I got home to her, I just remember feeling *so* miserable about everything. I was heading deeper and deeper into my depression and even though I was so glad (more like desperate) to have her there, I had lost my ability to see any good in the world (something I did well at hiding to those around me at college-a good use of my acting skills obviously).

But because she was my mum, I let my guard down big time, so every emotion I felt was etched all over my face, clear as day, for her to witness and also endure.

After seeing my distraught face, she sat me down and told me a story about her life prior to my birth that she'd never told me before and it was a big one-one I didn't see coming and looking back, I don't think I handled it very well at all.

She told me this story to try and reassure me that even when you're at your lowest low, there's still always hope and things really *can* turn around for the better.

But I didn't *choose* to hear that underlying message and instead I made *her* struggle all about *me* (and even though I'm cringing writing this) I think I might have pulled out the "You just don't understand what *I'm* going through" card as she tried her best to console me with her own vulnerable downtrodden to triumph story.

After another crying outburst (from me), I left for my last class of the day feeling confused, upset and even more inside my own head, running her story through my mind over and over again and letting the sadness and doom and gloom once again wash over me.

Totally *not* the point of her telling me it of course.

And I could have chosen differently that day and every other day for that matter.

I could have decided to listen first and foremost and realise that other people have *their* own struggles too, that perhaps this was a difficult thing for my mum to open up about and that I could have chosen gratitude for her trusting me with this story and focus on how we had just deepened our bond by sharing our vulnerable selves with each other...

But I didn't.

Because when you are depressed, you just don't.

At that time, I actually enjoyed the comfort my depression and anxiety gave me-not consciously, but on some subconscious level, it was keeping me safe and at least that felt familiar.

Of course, depression and anxiety *or* any other mental health issues are far from enjoyable. They suck, *a lot*.

But from my own *long* journey coming out the other side, I can look back and see that there's always a choice, whether we like it or not.

Perhaps you're experiencing feelings of depression or anxiety right now, or maybe you have in the past, or maybe you might at some point in the future...

I'd hasten to say that in today's world, more and more people are experiencing mental health problems than *ever* before.

But, the paralysing effects only come when we feel like we *aren't* in control anymore. Like we have to wait for some external force to stop these feelings inside of us, like we *would* try and come out of it, but it's beyond us...

I only say this now because I've been able to look back and make sense of my own scrambled mess. But at the time, I really didn't want to know any of this, mostly because of two reasons:

1. I felt like I wasn't in control of my emotions (depression/ anxiety) and so therefore, didn't know what I could do to feel better.
2. It couldn't be *that* simple.

But with hindsight and years and years of trial and error, I now know the following two things to be true:

1. We are the **only** ones in control of our emotions
2. It **is** that simple...

Now hear me out first before you slam this book shut in outrage!

These are two *very* simple, but *very* important lessons that I've learned coming out of the dark tunnel of doom and I want to pass them on to you in case they spark a feeling of hope inside for you too.

The fact that I always thought that life was happening *to* me, that other people *made* me feel a certain way, or that I was just *stuck* in my emotional state with no control over getting myself out of it whatsoever was, well, um, totally *not* true.

The reality we see is what we have each manifested for ourselves and our reactions to everything (and I mean *everything!*) dictate how this reality is viewed by us.

For example, imagine you wake up one morning and your alarm doesn't go off, so now you'll probably be late for class. So, you curse and you hurry and you faff around, only to find one Ballet shoe, then rush out of the door, ripping your jacket on the handle, tripping over your bag, scraping your knee and feeling very teary eyed and frustrated that life could be so cruel to you.

Now imagine another scenario, where you wake up and realise your alarm hasn't gone off, but you make a mental note to double check it before bed that night, then get ready as quickly as you can all whilst keeping a light attitude, deciding that if you won't make it to class for the warm up then it'd be a great idea to jog to the studio so you'll get there quicker *and* be warm when you arrive and thus your day goes on smoothly from there.

Do you see that we each get to choose what reality we are seeing in our day to day lives and how a simple shift in your thought process can dramatically change your whole day and the people in it too?

The fact that I thought *other people* were always to blame for me feeling rejected, sad or hurt was extremely naïve.

Let me ask you...if I were to tell you that you had a big nose, an awful top and that your walk wasn't as cool as mine, how would you react?

Would you *choose* to be offended?

Would you *choose* to be hurt?

Would you *choose* to retort with something equally as brutal?!

Or would you *choose* to shrug my comments off, realise that *"hurt people, hurt people"* and that it was more about *me* and the issues *I'm* going through, than about you at all and get on with your day just as cheery as you were before?

Some may call it taking the highroad.

And some may call it stupidity for allowing someone to say awful things to you...

But which option do you think will leave you feeling negative?

And which one will leave you feeling positive and in control of your life?

The fact of the matter is, we cannot pass the blame for anything in life because *we* are in charge of our reactions.

Even if someone throws a punch at you and it hits you right in the stomach...*they* (however much we want them to be) are not in control of what happens next.

I mean, you'll probably at least whimper even if you're great at taking responsibility for your actions/reactions, because, well it's a punch to your stomach and that would hurt. A lot.

But after that, would *you* take the highroad to maintain your inner peace, or would you start the blame game and ultimately enter into negativity and anger?

You always get to choose.

I didn't grasp this fact for a while. I'm talking like, a *long* time people.

So, when I was stuck in my dark tunnel, I was still convinced that other people were just adding to my misery and that I had *no* responsibility to take. I just believed that life was not working for me at the time somehow. Like it wanted to *intentionally* make me miserable and sad.

It wasn't until I'd been on anti-depressants for a year, decided to come off them because I *was* actually feeling a little better, then realised very quickly that my deep-rooted emotions hadn't gone away, that I realised that *nothing* and *no-one* could do this for me.

Which brings me on to my second point: It *is* that simple.

Feeling good is a choice.

As I have described above and as I'm sure you have witnessed in your own life, you can either be the person who screams at the poo on the wall, or you can go and get a sponge and clean it up...whilst whistling...and being grateful...and doing a shimmy.

Gratitude is the game changer.

A few years ago, my amazing dad had some very severe heart problems that seemed to appear out of nowhere.

Now, my dad is one of the fittest people you'd ever meet, he thrives off moving his body and keeping himself healthy, so this was a total shocker for everyone when it happened.

It was one of the worst times of my life and again, I didn't handle it very well at the time.

I focused on all the negatives I could find, the "What ifs?", the severity of the situation, the panic, the fear and the fact that I could quite possibly lose my hero, which was followed by sleepless nights, lots of tears, pointless distractions and a constant state of worry for his welfare.

But on the other hand, my dad was the complete opposite.

He had to deal with one thing after another after another; he couldn't breathe, his heart was failing, he had to leave his job that he loved because he was in hospital and recovery for so long, he had a Pacemaker fitted and then one of the wires immediately came out so he had to go straight back into surgery, he was bed bound (so no exercise) and he had a big, fat needle coming out of his neck...and this man, is absolutely terrified of needles.

But throughout all of it, he kept his positive demeanour.

He kept his humour.

And he stayed grateful, kind and loving.

I'm not so sure I would have been that brave, but my dad, he *chose* to focus on the good, he *chose* to live and he came out of that experience like a true Superhero.

You can have *nothing* to deal with, or you can have *everything* to deal with and I know from my *own* experience that you can feel depressed in both scenarios.

But from watching those around me and especially the people who have to contend with extreme situations or ailments, I know that you can also have nothing to deal with or everything to deal with and still *choose* to be happy and grateful.

Gratitude is the game changer.

Depression, anxiety or any other mental health issue are really just emotions, in the same way that happiness, love and joy are too.

Knowing this, it becomes easier to feel more in control of our internal state, because those negative feelings are just strong emotions that we are focusing on frequently.

Like the saying goes:

"What you focus on grows"
-Esther Hicks

I know for a fact that the more I focused on the negative things around me; the future, things I couldn't control or simply my lack of enthusiasm for life, *that* is what I saw and *that* is what grew right in front of my eyes shaping my reality day in and day out.

The more I felt depressed and anxious, the more I *was* depressed and anxious.

I used to give myself little challenges when times felt really tough and I'd *make* myself focus on every little good thing I could, just to see if it made any difference.

And guess what?

It made *all* the difference.

I would have glimpses into the magic of life and then the next day I'd be back into my dark tunnel with no light at the end.

I couldn't put two and two together at the time and realise that I'd actually *found* the secret to finding happiness and it wasn't in a pill or someone else, it was inside *me* all along.

When I focused on *every* good thing, all the love in the world and everything I had to be grateful for, I literally felt like I was living a magical life.

Then when I stopped or forgot to do that, I would experience the complete opposite and think that there was something wrong with me because I fell into my negative state again.

When in actual fact, the only thing that had gone 'wrong' was making a different *choice* that just didn't make me feel very good.

I'm going to be honest with you now.

This didn't work overnight for me. I know some people may portray otherwise, but I'm giving it to you straight okay?

I mean, when I was in a grateful, loving, happy state, I felt wonderful and life couldn't have been better.

But I hadn't made it a habit that just took over naturally yet. I needed more practice, every single day and this took years to develop.

And there are *still* days now where I'll *let myself* feel overwhelmed or down in the dumps, instead of being grateful. But when this does happen, the difference now is that I can quickly realise what's happening and make a better choice for myself, instead of riding the wave of darkness forever.

Gratitude is the game changer.

We have to work our minds *just* as much as we work our bodies.

You know when you've sat most of the day watching Netflix or been on your laptop for hours without moving? You feel stiff and lethargic and crave some sort of movement for your body to feel good again, don't you?

Well the same rules apply for your mind.

Your mind needs training daily too. It craves it, just as much as your body does.

We have to work on our mindset *every day* to make gratitude and positivity a habit that we can sustain, because it may be *simple* to go from depression to joy, but sometimes it's *not* easy.

You have to work at it daily unless you fancy entering the dark tunnel of doom and gloom again, so you've got to make it a habit in the same way that you wouldn't forget to eat or sleep each day.

The world we live in moves at an ever-growing rapid rate and sometimes we can feel like everything is on top of us, like there's no room to breathe and certainly *no* time for seeking out the stuff we have to be grateful for.

Which is why mindfulness is *key* for thriving in today's world.

Just in the same way that we can't be anxious and calm at the same time, when we are actively focusing on the good around us, we will *not* see the bad.

This is why being in nature is just so damn powerful.

We can breathe, we feel at peace and we have the time and space to focus on our immediate surroundings without being clouded by the rush of everyday life.

When was the last time you stopped and took in the world around you?

In any given moment, there is *so* much to be grateful for, even if you're not at first aware of it.

When I'd get myself into an anxious state, feel really low and focus on all the things that I hadn't got or done in my life, my lovely partner would help me to remember the little things that were right in front of me.

Things that we can often take for granted; like a really nice cup of tea, spending time with people we love, waking up in a house that's warm and safe, having food to eat, reading a great book, being outside and breathing in fresh air, getting cosy watching a movie, holding hands, hugs from people you love and being healthy.

It's *easy* to focus on the negative stuff; the things that aren't *quite* going right, the things that we haven't yet achieved or the circumstances we wish we *weren't* in.

That's easy.

But what's *simple*, is to *decide* to make a new choice.

To *choose* to be grateful.

Even though it might *feel* harder, because it's new territory, or you forget, or all you can see is pain...

Choose to be grateful anyway, because that simple decision will lead you to a life filled with magic and possibility.

Mind Love:

1. Make a list, right now, of everything around you that you can be grateful for. If you don't have access to a pen, your phone or laptop right now, make a mental note of everything around you that is positive and good.

2. When you start to feel down, depressed or anxious, stop and redirect your thoughts to gratitude.

3. Practice for one whole day being the most grateful person you know and see how you feel and how your life magically transforms.

CHAPTER 14

STEP OFF THE CRAZY TRAIN
AND OUT INTO BLISS LAND

When my anxiety was at its highest, I really didn't know what to do to soothe it or make it go the hell away.

Hindsight is a wonderful thing isn't it? I mean, sometimes I wonder why it exists, when having the knowledge we have years after could have *really* come in handy when we actually needed it most, right?!

But back then, I had *no* clue.

It felt paralysing at times to have this emotion that felt so out of my control coursing through my body, with (what I thought was) no way of making it stop.

Because the choices I felt I had at that time were to either carry on despite my pain and just endure it, or totally give up and end it all.

I chose the former of course...but don't get me wrong, it was hard.

Waking up every day feeling anxious, going through my day with anxiety bubbling up in my body and finding it hard to sleep at night because my mind would simply not rest and my body was on fire with this raging emotion.

I was so consumed with my anxiety and being so 'in my head' that I unknowingly but inevitably added to the intensity of it all.

I wondered if there would ever be a day when I woke up and felt free from this struggle.

That day felt like a million years away at the time and all my energy and might went into just 'making it through the day' without totally giving up at the end.

I never thought to make use of the gifts I'd been given... things we *all* possess inside us.

And one of them being, my breath.

My mum, being the brilliant Mental Health Practitioner that she is, used to tell me that you couldn't be anxious and calm at the same time. But being in a constant state of anxiety all the time, I just didn't believe her back then of course.

I remember when she used to sit with me and talk me through a relaxation she used at work and it would take me so long to just let go. I'd actually get the shakes because I felt so anxious trying to calm myself down. The opposite of what we were aiming for, I know.

But when I eventually did calm down (after many more guided relaxations) I realised that my mum was in fact right.

I *could* feel a sense of calm *without* my anxiety making an appearance at the same time.

It was a revelation and brought me such peace for that short amount of time I was in it. So, I started doing it every night before I went to sleep whilst I was at dance college when I couldn't have my mum's soothing voice right next to me guiding me through it.

The more I did it, the more I...well, I fell asleep before the CD had finished most nights.

So, basically, it worked.

But of course, life/rehearsals/watching Friends reruns got in the way and there wasn't always time (*I* didn't *make* the time) for an hour-long relaxation before bed, so ultimately, I didn't keep it up every day.

But even though my daily practice was a bit more sporadic (and sometimes non-existent), I learned a really important lesson and gift...that I *could* feel relaxed and I could make it happen quite quickly by using my breath.

As humans, we are designed to be curious, so using this in-built curiosity, I began to explore other forms of relaxation to help ease my pain that were a) safe and b) mostly free, I was a student after all.

Everything I tried worked to a certain extent, but usually only in the moment I was doing it. After the activity had ceased, I felt the same old anxiety creeping back in.

But funnily enough, the one thing that I could always come back to in any situation, was my breath.

And this is the thing that has had the most profound effect on reducing my anxiety and instilling an immediate sense of calm inside me.

I've never liked the London Underground. There, I said it.

It was a *huge* worry for me up until a few years ago, so I tried my best to avoid using it at all costs, even when I lived in London.

As you can guess, this didn't really work out very well and wasn't the most time productive idea I had, as it meant it would take twice as long to walk, catch two buses, then walk some more to my lessons.

So, when I *had* to take the Tube for teaching, going to class, an audition or just to meet up with friends, I panicked before I'd even left the house.

My biggest worry was that the Tube would get stuck in a black tunnel and I'd be trapped (kind of ironic as I was *already* trapped inside my own tunnel in my head at this time).

Now, if you're a Londoner, then you'll know that this happens quite often and is usually just because the train has to wait to proceed forward due to a red signal.

But, even though I, as a *fellow* Londoner at the time, knew this, I still had mini panic attacks whenever it happened.

I remember countless times having to get off at the next stop after the Tube had been stuck in a tunnel for about three minutes because I felt like I couldn't breathe, the time when I was on my way to meet my dad at Kings Cross Station and cried when I saw him because I'd been stuck on a Tube and felt like I couldn't feel my legs that had turned to jelly, when I *almost* started talking to the women next to me who looked like she might be open to soothing a crazy lady should the need arise (I mean, this is when I knew it had got *really* bad…talking to strangers on the Tube…I mean, it's *just not* done).

After countless situations like this, I finally decided that enough was enough and that I *had* to sort this issue out pronto.

So, I started using my breath and remembered my mum's wise word's in my head when the Tube would inevitably stop in a tunnel and I'd start to feel that ever familiar sudden panic rising up inside.

I practiced breathing slow, deep and full breaths.

I focused *only* on my breath and reminded myself that I was safe and everything would be okay.

Even though my anxiety and panic tried to remind me that they were ready and waiting to break free at any moment, I chose to *only* focus on my breath and see if I could dissolve this dilemma.

And it worked.

Now I'm not saying that those feelings don't come back from time to time when I'm riding any underground train, but now I have an immediate go-to tool to use every, single time.

And when I'm not riding the Tube breathing for Britain; I like to meditate...

I'm pretty sure *no one* does meditation in the same way and we all have the same thought of "Am I doing this right?", but what I've learned is that, it doesn't actually matter.

Meditation is about getting quiet, connecting to yourself and just 'being'.

And I'd like to hasten a guess that unless you're the Dalai Lama (and even then, I'm sure *he* has his off days too) you get distracted, perhaps a little bored, get a numb bottom or start thinking about your next meal.

But I'm going to tell you that it's *okay* to do that!

It's called a meditation practice and just like practicing dance, we never stop doing it. There is no end goal post to hit, it's an ongoing habit, just like showering or in some people's case, choosing *not* to shower.

Using meditation as a way to calm yourself and let go is fantastic, but don't then add the worry of 'not doing it right' or punishing yourself for drifting off a little in the middle of your session.

It's all okay.

I just decided one day that I would start, because I'd heard so many people raving about meditation that I wanted to see what all the fuss was about and I hoped that it could give me the inner peace I was searching for.

At first, I had all those common thoughts running through my head about not 'doing it right' and letting my mind take over and tell me what I had to do later on and that I needed to post that letter by 5pm etc...

But then, after some time, it got a little easier; my mind would still drift off and I'd still think about my to-do list, but I felt a little more relaxed at least.

Then skip to today and it's a *lot* easier, but I *still* get distracted from time to time and my mind will try and run the daily check list unless I consciously choose to stop it.

But what's different now, is that I am aware of it. Now, in no way am I 'enlightened' nor do I sit silently for twenty hours of the day cross legged in my bedroom.

I simply practice being still and quiet every day and I understand that my meditation and I, will never be 'perfect' together, so that gives me the freedom to drop the pressure and stress of having to 'do it right' and instead, I just get to sit for a while and feel relaxed.

I'm not going to give you a meditation to do, because as I've found, some don't work that well for me and some do, so I'm guessing you'll find the same-what works for me, may not work for you and vice versa.

But what I will say is this; do whatever feels good, for *you*.

There is no right or wrong way.

If you're feeling relaxed and at peace, then it's working, so keep doing whatever helps that feeling come about.

You'll know what feels good when you start playing around with different ways of being still and getting connected to yourself.

And be sure to remember that it is a *practice*; it's something we work on throughout our lives and it feels different to everyone, so finding something that you enjoy and can find peace from is what's most important.

If you find that sitting on a rock by the ocean staring at the horizon helps you to meditate, then go find that rock!

If you notice that walking through a forest gives you a feeling of peace and joy, then get those walking boots on!

If you love moving your body in ways that feel great, then let the rhythm take you!

And if you enjoy sitting cross legged on a mountain with your eyes closed, then, well just be sure you sit away from the edge...

Using our breath and meditation to calm ourselves and find inner peace and a bliss state are great tools to have in your belt and if you've got room for one more, then I've got just the tool to add to your collection.

Movement.

Did you guess it?

It's probably the oldest, most obvious one in the book (this book and also that well known phrase too) but that's because it *really* does work.

Moving our bodies feels amazing.

I know you hear me, right?

When we move, we can literally shake all negative feelings out of us and replace them with feelings of joy, euphoria and inner peace all at once.

When I was at dance college, I was moving, *a lot*. And despite my low self-confidence and overactive anxious mind, even if I was feeling really low, after moving my body I *would* feel a bit better.

And in this *one* particular class, I felt amazing.

You know that boy you go to school for? Well, this was the class I went to college for.

Every Wednesday morning I'd wake up actually excited (anxiety lessened briefly upon waking on *this* day) for my class at 8.30am.

Because *this* class, this class was my favourite and my teacher, well he was my idol at the time.

It was like I was a different person in this class-like the person I knew I was meant to be *full time*, but somehow just struggled to be any of the time. Except for this wonderful hour on a Wednesday morning.

I felt confident, sassy, capable and in full flow of my dancing passion.

Yep, every Wednesday morning, I got off the crazy train and stepped out into Bliss Land and it was *amazing*.

And what do you think my teacher's response was to me being my best self?

He noticed and encouraged me, he gave me attention and corrections to help me grow and he instilled even *more* confidence in my abilities through his nurturing and inspiring teaching methods.

Plus, his classes were always the most fun and different and I thrived off it all.

Moving my body in those classes felt as natural as breathing, only *way* sweatier!

I never wanted the lesson to end and couldn't wait for Wednesday to roll around once more, just so I could feel that way again. It was like my little fix, every week. And I just wanted more.

I had found something that truly touched my soul.

Perhaps you've felt this too?

All I know is this; I was a better human because of those classes. And I felt more like *me*, which is *always* a good thing.

In a dance college setting, all sorts of *things* can 'get in the way' of what you're actually there to do...which is of course, dance and move your body and become the best you can be at both.

And it's *much* more noticeable in this environment, because it's a full time endeavour, so all you do is eat, sleep and breathe dance every day.

The other *things* that I speak of, is all the *stuff* that goes on inside your head; mostly the negative chatter that just won't cease to stop talking.

So, from an outsider's perspective, you may think that a dancer's life at college is like life on a constant high because we're in our natural habitat, doing what we love *and* moving our bodies physically every day, therefore releasing a tonne of endorphins which make you feel great, right?

But from a dancer's perspective (and mine in particular), this isn't the whole truth.

Yes, we get to be physically active and move our bodies, but we also have to deal with all the *stuff* that goes on up *there* too.

We're not superhuman you know (even though that would be pretty cool if it were true...).

So, it's a constant battle between head and heart if you're anything like I was; consumed with all the negativity going on in my head, never fully allowing myself to enjoy the physical stuff my body was doing, but at the same time *desperately* craving the freedom of letting go.

My point is this, when you're feeling anxious, stressed or just blue, moving our bodies makes a *huge* difference in alleviating our pain points immediately.

But, to truly conquer these feelings and flip your life experience so that you have more positivity in your head, heart and reality than negativity, we must sort out all the *stuff* inside our heads too.

And as I so brilliantly demonstrated on a Wednesday morning in college; when the thoughts in our head are working *with* us, we feel confident, connected to ourselves and high as a kite as everything else we experience in life becomes a fun little ride too.

During *so* many other classes I had at college, I felt mostly anxious, scared or miserable because my mindset just wasn't working for me-I was constantly berating myself and generally not being my own best friend, so although the movement side *did* help, I missed out on

those utterly fantastic feelings I felt from Mr Wednesday's class, when I *was* being the best version of me.

And as you've witnessed from my story (promise I'm coming to a close now), it doesn't actually take much to switch from our negative state to an ultra-positive one.

I spent Monday, Tuesday, Some of Wednesday evening when the effects had worn off, Thursday, Friday, Saturday and Sunday in a state of anxiety, stress and not feeling good enough.

But on Wednesday morning, oh on Wednesday mornings, I felt awesome!

So, what changed?

Yep, you guessed it right again.

Me.

My mindset to be more precise.

Having got my mindset in check, I was able to experience life as the best version of me and my reality favoured this too.

It's hard to say "do this one thing and your life will be amazing", because it's a combination of *so* many things, many I've talked about throughout this book, but where to start?

Ah, well that's an easier one to answer, because everything starts with your mind.

Step off the crazy train running through your mind, redirect the track (your thoughts) to Bliss Land and you're already halfway there!

Mind Love:

1. If you start to feel anxious, stop, take a deep inhale, then exhale slowly. Focus *only* on your breath and keep doing this until your anxiety starts to ebb away.

2. Remember that you can't be anxious and calm at the same time, so find activities that help you to feel calm and in flow, so you can make these your go-to when you need to swap stress for serenity.

3. Practice being still, in whatever way that manifests for you and remember that whatever you choose, is right for you.

4. Swap your negative self-talk for inner conversation that's actually going to make you feel good-you are amazing. Tell yourself this on repeat.

5. "Shake it off" like Tay Tay.

CHAPTER 15

THERE'S HOMEWORK EVERY NIGHT... AND *YOU* ARE THE CASE STUDY

Being a human, let *alone* a dancer, is a lifelong learning curve.

You're never 'done' and you never 'get there', because there are *always* lessons to be learned about life and the people in it (including yourself).

When I was younger, I didn't really know myself very well.

Which seems like a weird sort of thing to say, seeing as you're with yourself all the time, but the truth is, I didn't.

I didn't realise that like Shrek, I *too* was an onion, with layer upon layer of fascinating quirks, values and most importantly, emotions.

Oh, the emotions.

Do you remember back in school, when you were given homework so you could *really* get to grips with what you'd been learning in class and cement that into every crevasse of your brain?

Well, YOU are your homework for life (sorry to be the one to tell you it's not over) and it takes daily discipline and an avid curiosity to explore the many layers of your *own* onion.

I can't begin to tell you all the things I've found out about myself over the years, because, well that alone would fill this book (and also a sequel no doubt).

But back in my school days, all throughout dance college *and* most of my early twenties, I didn't think I *needed* to find out anything.

And the thought of sitting with myself, being alone with my thoughts or making time for personal growth or development didn't even cross my mind, or if it did, it probably freaked me out and I quickly ushered that thought away because I was *so* uncomfortable being alone or having to do 'the work' on myself.

When I broke my big toe during my second year at college, I was mortified.

It was coming up to showtime and rehearsals were fully underway and I would now have to miss this experience and forfeit all the opportunities I'd been given to perform in the show.

I went into full on despair mode as I picked up my crutches and consequently travelled home in the car with my parents, where I would spend the rest of term (and summer holidays) either sitting or lying down and most definitely *not* dancing.

But a part of me felt relieved and like a weight had been lifted off my shoulders.

It was strange and I decided to ignore these emotions until many years later, because as I said, back then, sitting with myself and really getting to know what I wanted or who I was, was *terrifying*.

The breakage of my toe happened at the same time as my flatmate turmoil and looking back, was actually my ticket out of it all.

I was *so* desperate for a way out, I literally couldn't see my next move, so the Universe, God, or my higher self, jumped in to lend a helping hand.

Although it was a very, VERY painful experience to go through (I'd never broken a bone before that) it meant that my battle with my roomies could finally finish. I was free to leave that situation and never come back.

At the time, this wasn't even crossing my mind consciously of course.

As I said, I was mortified when I couldn't take part in the end of year show...my second-year show! I'd never get another one of those.

Plus, I'd been chosen (along with only three others from my year) to perform in Mr Wednesday's routine with the third-year students and *that* was basically the highlight of my year, which was now coming to a crashing end.

After resting my toe and spending what seemed like *forever* in isolation, it was time to go back to college for my third and final year.

By this time, I had secured a new home with my lovely friend and all was well when I returned, as I was able to leave the mess I'd been involved in behind me.

Upon reflection of this whole event, I realised I had actually peeled back a layer of my onion and learned a little bit more about myself.

I had subconsciously been wanting an escape during that time and so through (painful) events, I was granted one.

I was on the verge of something I'm not even sure of and this 'accident' allowed me to take some much-needed time away to recentre myself and be around people who really *did* love and care for me.

I was able to see that everything happens for a reason and that I was one powerful mother trucker for being able to manifest a way out for myself.

I also learned that I was extremely stubborn and would never, ever quit.

Which actually, at that time, probably wouldn't have been a bad choice, but I was *so* dedicated to my craft that I would never have admitted defeat and would have rather suffered and stay stubborn in my loyalty to dance, than take time away to make my self-care a priority again.

So, instead of me admitting I wanted out, I was *forced* to go by external circumstances (that I had subconsciously manifested of course).

It was the best scenario really, because, how could I argue with a broken toe?!

Even though that period of my life (which now seems like a bit of a blur) was hard going and extremely testing, I learned valuable lessons about myself; things that I needed to work on (or work out) and things that I learned were positive strengths inside me which I could then build upon.

That was one of the first times I really dug a little deeper into my psyche and ultimately, peeled back my first layer.

And the thing is, peeling layers is kind of like eating Pringles, once you pop, you can't stop!

There were onion peels left, right and centre after that...I'd started my journey on unearthing a great mystery...myself... and I couldn't stop.

It can be *so* scary to take the time to really get to know yourself.

Especially, if you're struggling with any kind of heavy emotion like anxiety or depression.

The last thing you want to do is go *further* inside your head, when all it seems you do is live there full time anyway.

But I promise you this, even though it can feel *mighty* uncomfortable, it may even make you feel uneasy or sick to your stomach to stop and start peeling layers, after the first one is gone, it gets *so* much easier.

After you *decide* that YOU need to be your main priority in life and it'd be well worth your time and energy getting to know *everything* you can about yourself, life gets a whole lot easier.

The only way you'll be able to get to where you want to go is if you keep growing and expanding your comfort zone, keep listening to your instincts and intuition and get *really* uncomfortable first.

It's kind of fun though, getting to know yourself-because you learn a lot and you realise that you *are* in fact, much cooler and more awesome than you ever thought.

You also get to direct your life the way you want, create positive opportunities for yourself and generally have a great time along the way.

Before the age of about twenty-seven, I had never really taken myself out.

I'd gone shopping alone, or driven to places on my own, but I'd never taken myself *out*.

Like, on a date with myself.

Ever.

It sounded and felt *so* weird and uncomfortable but I knew that I would inevitably have to do it if I wanted to grow and expand my comfort zone again.

I remember feeling *so* out of my safety net, feeling like *everyone* was looking at me and judging, like my face was on fire from embarrassment at sitting in this café *alone* drinking my smoothie as quickly as I could and hoping no one would talk to me and ask if I'd been stood up.

Err, mortifying!

Then ironically, I began to do it more because I started to quite enjoy it and as you're probably now aware, the more you do something, the less scary it becomes.

And the same goes for self-dating.

So, I practiced it a lot.

Taking myself out to cafes for drinks, then gradually building up to ordering a little snack or two...

Then came the big one for me.

I took myself out for dinner...ALONE!

Then swiftly after that milestone, I went to see a Broadway show alone and after many countless dates with myself of varying activities...I flew and stayed in Bali by myself.

And each and every time, I learned a little bit more about myself; about my triggers and fears and how I could overcome each of them and it became easier as my confidence and self-esteem grew.

Something I most *definitely* wasn't expecting to learn, as a once exceptionally shy girl, was that I *loved* dating myself and spending time alone.

It's something I make time for regularly now and I can definitely feel it if I don't. I get a little strained or stressed and I actually *crave* my alone time.

If you're reading this and having a full-on sweat fest, then please rest assured that you don't have to jump in and book a flight to Bali on your own to start self-dating!

Just start.

Start small and build up from there.

I completely get that the first time is probably going to feel *unbelievably* nauseating and there's a high chance that your body will try and hold you back from walking out of your house or opening the café door, or booking the cinema ticket for one, but you can *totally* do this.

It's time to reassure yourself, *by* yourself.

When we spend time getting to know ourselves (alone) *we* have to do all the talking and keep the conversation positive and upbeat. *We* have to treat ourselves with kindness and ultimately after a few dates, *we* have to fall in love with *ourselves*.

It's just like any other relationship, except you're in the one with yourself for life, so it'd be a good idea to invest some quality time making it a damn good one to be in.

Don't you think?

Along with self-dating, another good habit to adopt is journaling.

When we write down all the thoughts in our head and read them back, we get to see the jumbled mess in a more coherent form and thus, start to make sense of what we're actually all about.

There doesn't have to be a structure if you don't want and at the beginning, just think of it like writing a diary, except you probably won't start your entry with "Dear diary", it'll be more like a random collection of thoughts like Adrian Mole.

We have *so* many thoughts in a day and I don't know about you, but if there's a way to get some of them out and make sense of them, I'm up for doing it.

If you're new to journaling and you're cringing and also slightly scared to think what kind of jargon is going to come out of your head and on to the paper, don't sweat it!

We all have to start somewhere and basically, you can either start with this or take yourself out of the house for a coffee...yeah, that journaling malarkey doesn't seem so bad now does it!

When we're unsure of who *we* are and can't see the mud through the puddles in our minds, how can we *possibly* get what we want out of life?

If we're not willing to get uncomfortable for a little while *now* and take the time to learn about our own needs and expectations for ourselves, then, when *will* we?

How long are you willing to wait to feel amazing and live a life you love?

It all starts with *you.*

Once we begin tuning in, listening carefully and making time for our own growth, we hear *so* many calls from inside which can clearly direct us forward on to a path that we love.

When we stay distant, disconnected and disinterested in ourselves, we stay stuck.

If you thought that you were through with the homework nightmare, think again.

Your studies have only just begun!

Soul Love:

1. Take yourself out. On a date. Alone. And enjoy yourself! Things are about to get good.

2. Grab a pen and paper and do a brain dump of everything that's in your mind. Then repeat that the following day and the next and so on; read it back if you want to, or simply see how you feel after releasing your thoughts.

Make yourself a priority-get curious about *who* you are and *why* you do things the way you do...who's the person staring back at you in the mirror and what are they trying to tell you?

CHAPTER 16

DO IT FOR THE LOVE...
NOT FOR THE LIKES

When was the last time you actually asked your bestie how they were with a quick text, phone call or shock horror... in person meet up, instead of checking their stories on Instagram or Facebook to see what they were up to?

I'm not shaming you, because the fact is, we've *all* done it.

That's what the world encourages today; we're all *more* connected than ever before thanks to the Internet and yet *so* many of us feel hugely disconnected, dissatisfied and lonely because of that same thing.

We've become *so* consumed in the online world, that human interaction isn't made to be a priority anymore, but the need for it, is still absolutely necessary.

The online world is like emotional fast food as my partner says, which I think sums it up excellently; you want everything now, it's fast paced and you feel good as soon as you taste it, but not long after, it leaves you feeling heavy, lethargic and never really *full*, so you need to do it again.

And so, the cycle continues.

I've talked a lot about social media already in this book and the pressures of comparison, but because it is such a *huge* part of our society and daily life now, I feel that there's still more to be said for this strange phenomenon.

I'm sure you have your own opinion about social media and it's probably a bit of a mix, like with most people.

On the one hand it's great because of A, B and C, but on the other hand it's not because of X, Y and Z.

Whether you have a business page, a personal blog or a mismatch of everything, a lot can be gauged from the content you put out for the world to see.

I remember a time, many years ago, when I'd perform in shows with my local dance school and we'd take a few group photos on a set of steps or on stage in our cool costumes before the curtain call, so we could remember the event and stick it in our scrapbooks, or make a funny birthday card for our friend with an incriminating backstage shot on the front!

Back then, there was no pressure to post minute by minute snapshots of our lives and all the non-consequential stuff that would make up a really addictive, albeit hideously boring reality show.

Thank goodness.

I'm so grateful I got to experience those precious moments *without* the pressure back then. I do *not* envy those young'uns today, I can tell you that for nothing.

We lived in a blissful state of this thing called 'being present', maybe you've heard of it?!

All jokes aside, when the big boom of social media struck, it had mixed reactions then and still does.

But one thing it does do, is give us all a creative outlet where we can express ourselves, play and showcase what we can offer the world.

As a dancer, this can be a great thing, because (copyright restrictions aside-err hello, bane of my life!) we can literally showcase our skills and abilities through posting dance clips, our choreographic creations and impromptu improvisations in the park and reach thousands of people within minutes.

So, not only is this a creative outlet, but it also can lead to work opportunities because we are increasing our potential of being seen by people all over the world, who may want to hire us.

It's like having a video CV always available for anyone to see what we can do and *that* is priceless when you're your own boss.

I adore watching other people's dance videos online and seeing how they individually express themselves through movement. It's fascinating to me and is a pleasurable experience to watch other people create art they love.

What also really stands out to me, is when people post with an agenda.

This is the other side of social media and something I know *I* have done in the past to some extent and I'm guessing *you* or someone you know has done it too...

It's the kind of post that is put into the world with the expectation of some kind of self-indulgent return, meaning, they're doing it for the likes, instead of the love.

It's the 'accidental' shot where they are caught off guard, the 'one Emoji says it all' tag line and the highly edited 'I just woke up like this' posts.

Bear in mind that *almost* everyone you know is on social media, so that just increased the likelihood of every potential employer seeing your feed and weighing up whether they have a part that you could fill. Or not.

And your feed, as I said, is telling them everything they need to know from the last picture you posted.

Whatever you may have heard about the dance industry, just know *this* to be true...people want to work with *nice* people.

They do *not* want to work with someone who appears to be self-obsessed or has an agenda that places her/himself a higher priority than being a team player.

Just imagine it for yourself; let's say there's a group of six of you working together on a show, how much harder is it going to be if one or two of the group are only interested in their own gains, rather than that of the team?

People want to work with people who are relatable, friendly and reliable. And that's a fact.

But somehow, we don't believe this to be true and always think we have to do, show and *be* more to really be enough or what people want.

We worry that posting an unedited picture (without hash tagging *#nofilter*) will be enough...

We worry that a video of us dancing on our iPhone with gym clothes on won't be aesthetically pleasing enough...

We worry that *we* are not enough...

But the fact here is this; our lives matter and we *are* enough.

Imagine for a moment that you're with your friends, family or partner and having a lovely time doing something enjoyable.

What does that scene look like?

Smiling faces?

Hugs and kisses?

Laughter?

Engagement and connection?

Memories being made?

Now answer me this...

Is there a filter on that picture in your head?

Do you need to airbrush anything out?

Is the resolution high enough?

They're just not important right!

So, why is it that we can enjoy our real-life interactions and activities without the need to heighten, brighten and illuminate them, but sharing these *same* moments online becomes a whole other story?

We assume that 'just us' without endless filters and airbrushing is not enough.

But *that* is exactly what people love and need more of.

The unretouched, relatable human who *is* flawed but still irrevocably beautiful and magnificent, just as they are.

As technology continues to develop and we move forward as a society with it, it would make sense to *use* it to our advantage, rather than become overwhelmed or stressed when hearing the words 'social media'.

We can't stop this progression, but we *can* choose how we deal with it.

If you use social media currently and you feel pressure or a kind of responsibility to post on there for whatever reason, I'd urge you to take a step back, even step off the crazy train for a while and live your real life first and foremost.

The world will not stop if you don't post a picture of your morning selfie or cat, nor will it change much if you do.

If you have something you want to share, share it because *you* want to, not because you think you *should*.

If you love making art in some form or another and want to share that love with others, then be my guest and do it from a place of love, rather than a place of 'waiting for the likes and comments to come rolling in so you can feel better about yourself'.

But also know that it's okay *not* to share your life with the world too.

There's so much to be said for real life interactions and connections, so cherish those when you have them and don't let the pressure of having to document it take over and ruin these precious moments.

I've been on both sides of the fence for this and I'm still learning too.

But what I know for sure is that when we fill ourselves and our lives with lots of the good stuff, we become so involved with living, *rather* than with posting or scrolling.

And then ultimately, when we *do* post, it comes *without* a motive or a need for validation and instead it comes from love of living our real lives and sharing this love with others.

Everyone wants to be seen and heard. It's a natural human need.

But there's a difference between seeking love and sharing it.

I still stand by my belief that having a way to showcase your talents and skills online is a remarkable thing for everyone (especially dancers) and particularly, when you can mostly do this for free too.

It's a new gateway for artists to have creative freedom and express themselves, where perhaps they might not have had the chance in the past or in every day, real life circumstances.

So, notice when you next use social media and the emotions behind the post.

Are you excited to share your picture/video/work with the world because you're super proud of it/think it will be useful for someone/or just enjoyed making it?

Or are you posting because you're feeling a bit low and need a validation pick-me-up?

Notice the difference and understand your reasoning behind it. Then act accordingly.

Remember when you first tried something and loved it?

Perhaps it *was* dancing.

And that love grew and grew and you just couldn't get enough of it?

Your soul felt all warm and squidgy, like a little fire had been lit inside you.

You noticed those loving feelings every time you participated in that activity and your love only deepened over time.

Remember that?

Sometimes it's hard to describe that feeling of love for something that is your passion, whether that is dancing, sailing, writing, climbing, flying, reading, travelling or whatever sets your soul alight.

But for me, Billy Elliot got pretty close when he said it felt like electricity.

It courses through your veins and your whole body comes alive.

And there was a time when you did that thing you loved, *for* the love, not the likes.

It's a strange one, really. And I often think about how our children's children will look back at our world today and laugh at the nonsensicalness of it all.

But then again, perhaps they won't? Who *knows* where technology and social media will be by then!

But whilst we are still alive and kicking in the midst of this technological upgrade and surrounded by everyone vying for attention and love, we may as well have some fun and show the *real* us, right?

Imagine a world that only existed in real life...it's funny to think how that's hard to imagine, when just a few short years ago, that *was* the reality.

But imagine it anyway.

What would you do?

How would you live your life?

How would you feel?

And what in the world would happen to all of those selfie sticks?!

We'd all have a lot more storage on our phones though wouldn't we?

I've got nothing against a good selfie, but the impetus behind it, is what I'm making a point about.

If you went to a dance class and just participated in that class, without pictures, videos or boomerangs...how would that feel?

If no one else but the people in that room were involved, would it still have been worth it? Does it still count? Would you enjoy it as much if it wasn't shared with the world online?

I want to share something important with you that I have experienced in my life that I think may help you in your quest for happiness...

Your self-worth, happiness and peace cannot be found online.

Every time I felt anxious or depressed, I used social media as my drug.

It was a distraction (and a pretty one at that) a place for validation and somewhere I thought I could get inner peace and connection from.

But I couldn't have been more wrong.

I was using it for all the wrong reasons and I just couldn't stop.

And every time I wondered why I didn't *feel* any better?

You don't have to do much to 'show up' online do you?

I mean, choose a picture, write some words and press post. Easy peasy. Then all you have to do is wait; wait for the comments, the likes and the validation to sweep over you and make you feel all warm and appreciated for a short while.

Until you need to do it again.

But showing up in life, now that's a bit more challenging.

But that's exactly what *I* needed to do...engage with life and the people in it, rather than depending on the internet to give me what I needed.

Today, I remind myself that the internet is there for *my* use only, there are no demands on me from anyone and should I *choose* to engage, I know I've made that choice based out of love and *not* fear *or* for the likes.

It's a great tool for business and I appreciate that no end, but if ever I'm feeling a little anxious, I spend time on self-care rather than on scrolling and it makes *all* the difference.

The honest truth is; life is short, so do what you love, act from a place of love and have a lot of fun along the way. Make art if your heart calls you to, create a business that you love building, have amazing experiences that leave you giddy and make your priority the love of *doing* them, *not* the act of sharing them.

That part is always just a fun little secondary action.

Mind Love:

1. Keep a check on your social media screen time. You can set this up on your phone, or just keep a little notepad with the timings on. Check back after seven days and add it all up. If it's more than you thought (and I can almost guarantee it will be...because when *I* did this, it almost made me fall over) then perhaps see if you can bring that number down the next week and then the week after and so on.

2. Ask yourself if there is something you'd like to pursue in your life right now? Meditate on this and see what answers come up for you. Removing distractions like social media can allow space for our desires to come up to the surface and be heard.

3. Always be aware *why* you are using social media. Is it for fun? For love and connection? For validation? For a creative outlet? Become aware and act responsibly.

4. Show a little more *you* and a little less highlight reel. The things we often try and hide for fear of judgement or rejection are usually the things that others relate to also. Remember, it's okay to be real.

CHAPTER 17

PREPARE FOR SUCCESS

I remember the first time I experienced manifestation for myself and immediately thinking that I was in The Truman Show, because how could anything be so freaky as to come into my reality that quickly just by thinking it?!

I was lying in my bed in that wonderful between sleep stage, half asleep and half thinking about my schedule for college that day, when I let my mind go into a little daydream (or what may also be known as a visualisation).

It wasn't very long, but being a visual type with a playful imagination, it was *extremely* vivid and clear as day as if it was in fact happening in real life that very moment.

I had Ballet that same morning, like every morning at college and I just wanted a fun class with this particular teacher that day as I was feeling a little sleepy and tired in my body.

She wasn't the scariest of the lot, but let's just say, well you still wouldn't want to cross her if she hadn't had her morning cigarette or coffee.

So, with my fun class in mind, I let myself imagine being in that lesson, putting the barres away early and coming to the centre of the studio to do some exercises that required us to let go a bit and really move our bodies freely.

I pictured this one move, that I don't think I'd ever even tried doing myself in real life but had seen somewhere before and it had obviously made an impression on me as I was still thinking about it.

In my head, I saw my reflection in the mirror doing it with gusto and grace all at once, as if I had done it a thousand times.

I felt alive, it was fun and I was smiling and open in class instead of hiding away praying that no one would see me.

This visualisation didn't last very long as I said, but I really *felt* it with all of my body.

I then got up, got ready and made my way to class as usual, not really thinking anything more of it.

When I arrived at the studio, just like normal, we took turns to take out the barres and line up, whilst practicing a few exercises before our teacher arrived.

Then when she came in, we started with our Plies, then onto a Tendu exercise, then she told us to put away the barres (which we were a little annoyed about because they were heavy and cumbersome and basically, we couldn't be bothered after just doing it ten minutes prior!) and then we were told to come into the centre.

I was starting to feel a little odd, because I felt like I'd already lived this scene before and I knew exactly what happened next in my head.

And would you Adam and Eve it…the next thing we did, was the exercise I'd visualised in my head earlier that morning that I had *never* done before except inside my mind and also, we had never actually done in hers or any of the other Ballet classes before. Ever.

I remember having a little laugh to myself as I stood in the centre and so there stayed my smile for the remainder of the lesson, just like my visualisation!

We had a great time; it was fun, light and I felt that for the first time in a long time, I was dancing freely. Not worrying about all the technicalities and alignment requirements, but just dancing because it felt good to move that way.

After class, I remember thinking that *I* had made that happen. Then I freaked myself right out and began to think that I was living in some sort of bubble where the world revolved around me, because how *else* could that have even occurred?

Luckily for me, my mum was *all* for the woo woo and had books upon books on visualisation and manifestation that would take me literally years to get through.

So, instead of waiting ten years to complete her book collection and finally feel enlightened on this subject, I just rang her up and asked her if she could explain a little more about what had just happened.

I'm so glad that I did, because she told me all about these coaches who train athletes to practice running their races in their minds prior to the actual event (as well as physical training) to get amazing results and ultimately win their races.

This was very interesting to me.

They won the race in their mind first, then consequently, they won the race in reality afterwards.

I visualised this dance move in my head first, then it became my reality. Hmm, I was starting to see a pattern.

Obviously these two examples are at two ends of the spectrum, but they both still display using visualisation, manifestation and the law of attraction to get the desired end result.

I was so smug about what I had achieved that day, but unfortunately at the time, I hadn't strengthened those particular mindset muscles to continue playing with my visualisations and create even more of what I wanted.

So, I went back to creating a lot of unwanted outcomes instead. Not consciously of course, but not a great use of my mind, I must admit.

Now, even though I had experienced first-hand, the powers of my mind, I still *chose* to sink back into thinking that the events of my life were happening *to* me and I was powerless in changing them because this was easier and it meant nothing had to change.

Perhaps you've been in the same boat?

I mean, it's very easy to do isn't it?

It avoids taking responsibility for our lives and instead gives us *someone* or *something* else to blame.

I know that sounds harsh, because *why* would anyone choose to just *let* rubbish things happen to them over and over again if there was another way?

Obviously we wouldn't do this if we *knew* there was another way right?

But the truth is, it takes perseverance, dedication and ongoing discipline to retrain your mind to think in another way. To retrain your mind to a point where you actually *create* your current reality and know that all that is happening, is actually *for* you instead of happening *to* you.

This may *sound* like a lot of work, but guess what...if you dance, you've already got these necessary qualities inside you right now to pull this off! Because what are the biggest traits needed in the dance world? That's right; perseverance, dedication and discipline.

Good news, right?

And the other *great* news, is that anyone can do this-all it takes is for you to stay dedicated and disciplined every single day, for the rest of your life. Easy.

I know what you're thinking though, that doesn't *sound* very easy-it sounds like a lot of work that would take a lot of time and you've just got *too* many other things to think about right now.

I get it, I really do.

But I'd urge you to ask yourself-would creating your reality and manifesting everything your heart desires be better than thinking that life is just *happening* to you and everything is out of your control and therefore life is hard and causes you pain...?

If the answer is yes, then definitely keep reading.

If the answer is no, um, well, maybe for your own sake and sanity-keep reading also...

I spent years believing that everything was out of my control, life was hard, I never got any breaks, people were rude and mean and *I* was a nice person, so why the hell was my life not where I wanted it to be?

But all the time I believed that, I was busy manifesting it too.

Re-read that sentence again.

You get me?

So, by concentrating on all the negativity going on around me, I was just encouraging more of that *to* me and life was very obliging and aided me all the way, because that's what life and the Universe does-it helps things happen *for* you.

No matter whether they're positive or negative.

That's always *your* choice to determine.

And because I'd unknowingly chosen to let the negative side of the battery be on top, I had ultimately got into an endless cycle and was *so* ready to break out of it.

The thing is, I know how hard it is to believe something when all you see is the darkness. How can there *possibly* be light at the end of the tunnel when it just looks black-it must be a trick or at least, a *very* long tunnel.

I know that being told that life *can* be an amazing ride and that the Universe really *does* have your back can sound like utter rubbish, if all you're experiencing is pain, sadness and despair.

I know that to believe in something unseen and perhaps unfamiliar can feel so alien and scary and hard but...

I'm going to ask you to do it anyway.

When I was at my lowest low, the time *after* I thought I was at my lowest of course...if I even smelt a whiff of positivity from someone, it would make me want to punch a wall because *I* was not experiencing this blissful life that they raved about and then I'd continue to focus on how unfair it was for others to feel happy and *not* me.

What I misunderstood at the time, was that all it would take for me to experience life as a gift rather than a burden, was to make a choice.

To *choose* happiness and every good thing.

If I had consistently chosen this for myself when I felt so desperately low (even though it would have *felt* extremely hard to do at the time) my reality and my demeanour would have completely transformed as if overnight.

But I didn't do this.

Not for years.

Because in my mind, I was waiting for *something* or *someone* to come and save me from myself and make everything better, just like my parents and older siblings had done for me when I was a child.

But again, I had it all back to front.

And I'm going to tell you something I have learned from my years of experiencing the highs of life and the very dark lows...

No one is coming.

And here's another corker...

YOU are the answer.

I'm not sure why we doubt ourselves and our abilities so much as humans. We tend to think that someone *else* has all the answers, that someone *else* is more able and that someone *else* will come and take us away from our lonely darkness.

So, just for a minute, stop right now and take a moment to appreciate all that *you* are.

If this feels hard to do, do it for even longer!

The truth is that *you* are the only person in the whole world who can change your life, course correct your path and inevitably 'make' yourself happy.

I know we hear all the time from people how an event, a book, a person or an experience completely *'changed their life'*, but the fact is, it didn't. Not *really*. It may have *added* greatly to their state, but what changed their life, will always have been them.

Because *they* are the only ones to do that for themselves, just as *you* are the only one to do it for *yourself.*

Isn't that a relief though, really?

Isn't that like the magic pill, wizarding spell, fairy Godmother you've been searching for all these years?

It's all down to *you*.

And what great news that is-because now you can stop searching, now you can feel at peace and now you can trust yourself to be the guide for your own life.

When all of this *finally* began to sink in for me, I think I protested a little with a bit of:

"But why do *I* have to be the answer?"

"I don't think I can do it"

"I wish *you* could do it for me"

"But it's just so *hard* to keep it up every day"

"What if I get it wrong and it doesn't work for *me*?"

"What if there's another secret that I haven't been told that's *really* the answer?"

And so on.

It was like having an on/off relationship with life for probably, oh a good few years!

I battled and fought hard, I'll give myself that credit.

But when life got totally fed up with my resistance, it gave me *a lot* of signs to just stop it already.

For the longest time, all I heard, saw and felt inside me were the words "Let Go" and *so* many times I just couldn't do it. I didn't know how to do it. I didn't *want* to do it.

I'd spent most of my life in this fear based mentality, thinking that my job in life was to walk forward and take whatever happened to me as 'part of the gig' and (in my eyes) I'd 'wasted' years of my life worrying, doubting and being depressed, which was absolutely horrible-but in some ways a new type of comfort blanket for me at the time and to give that up for something unknown, well that was extremely scary because it was new and different.

When I eventually decided that life *without* struggle and stress actually sounded like a better path than the one I was currently on...I let go.

And I'm not going to lie to you, because let's face it-we're forever friends now after being bound by this book, so I'll save you the 'and she lived happily ever after' and give you the *real* dealio, which comes quite close ironically.

After *finally* deciding to *choose* life, instead of fight against it, I didn't become this enlightened Guru who spends her time silently sitting cross legged on a mountain surrounded by goats.

I just became...more of who I knew I was always meant to be. As cheesy as that may sound, it's undoubtedly true.

And wonderful!

And a relief!

By letting go, choosing to live life on purpose and *create* my own reality, I was really *choosing* myself.

But this also doesn't mean that once you decide to let go and trust, that everything you want just *magically* appears at your doorstep.

No, I'm afraid Britney was right, *"You better work"*.

This isn't a 'one time only' scenario, where you just wake up and all your dreams have come true (unless you wake up at Disney, then…).

This is the path to success in all areas of your life and the first step on that yellow brick road, is *choosing* it.

The next one is to *keep* choosing it, then the next step is to keep choosing it *again* and so on, until you eventually get to the end of the road and follow it up to the rainbow in the sky.

To prepare for your success right now, all you have to do is decide.

Are you going to struggle and fight with life, believing that you have *no* control over anything and that nothing ever goes your way and you always end up doing Petit Allegro in every Ballet class?

Or, are you going to let go, believe that you *are* in fact very powerful and create your life exactly how you want it, Floor Barre and all!

The choice is yours and it's an ongoing question from life waiting for you to answer it each day.

If you choose life today and tomorrow things turn a bit wibbly, just choose life again as soon as you've regained your thoughts and keep repeating *this* cycle until you're doing it in your sleep.

It really doesn't matter how many times you think you might 'slip up' or 'make a mess of it all' or 'let the poop hit the fan' as long as you keep choosing yourself, keep saying yes to life and remember that no one can do it, but you.

Mind Love:

1. Practice using your mind to your advantage right now! Imagine something you'd like to see, or a scenario you'd like to happen, then close your eyes and picture it exactly as you'd like it to be-add colour, smells, feelings, as much detail as you can and really *feel* it. Keep at it, until it feels real. Then let it go. Let go of expectation. Let go of control. Just believe and know that it'll show up when it's meant to and stay aware and open to it coming to you.

2. Decide to say *yes* to yourself and to your one, precious life.

CHAPTER 18

MAKING A LIFE OUT
OF YOUR LIVING

For as long as I can remember, all I ever wanted to do was dance.

I was born with a big lump on my head (Conehead style... *shiver runs down my spine*) from all the wriggling (dancing) I was doing on my way out.

Luckily the bump went away but my passion for dance only grew stronger.

There are old videos of me dancing to my mum's fitness DVD's, bobbing along to Fraggle Rock (am I showing my age?) and dancing to Michael Jackson songs *on tape* (how about now?) in my bedroom with my cousins.

But the first time I *really* knew that I wanted to be a dancer when I grew up, was when my parents took me to see Cats the Musical when I was six years old.

Since that day, I soaked up as much as I could about how I could perform on stage like that, inevitably playing the White Cat as my ultimate goal and mission in life.

But with my shy personality, the whispers about the dance world that I'd allowed myself to believe in rather than *in* myself and not much in the way of being a rebel with my methods, it just never sort of happened that way.

I stuck to the rules. I played the game and I did it *really* well.

Never straying out of line, always doing what I was told and obeying the rules, just like a good girl.

But the thing is, sometimes things can get outdated or aren't energetically right or just don't end up making you very happy.

But I *"carried on regardless"* as The Beautiful South would say and didn't divert my attention for a second and at the same time, never allowed my unique creativity or ideas to fully blossom either.

Let me explain a little more.

Let's say your chosen career is to become a doctor.

So, you go to University and do all those many, many years to qualify as a doctor, presuming that at the end of your education, you'll probably get a job as a GP or a specialist in a hospital setting.

Perhaps this is what you've been told doctors do, or what you've experienced so far, or maybe it's what is expected of you from others or even yourself?

So, you don't stray from the path laid out and you follow the system and structure to a T.

But what about all of the other doctors who aren't in those roles?

The ones who fly overseas to work with Doctors Without Borders, or set up their own practice, or who write a book, or contribute to health magazines, or become crowd doctors or who volunteer in their community?

Sometimes, we can become blind sighted to the abundance of opportunities and experiences on offer to us, because we are *so* fixated on just *one* specific path that we think is the be all and end all for our career and life.

But it's just not so.

Of course, if being a GP or working in a hospital environment is what your heart truly desires, then by all means, go for it!

But if you're just doing something because it seems like the only way to do it, think again.

In today's world, we have more options available to us than ever before and sometimes this can feel overwhelming, but it can also feel exhilarating-it just depends on your point of view.

Now let's take dancing as our chosen career focus and I'll share my *own* experience of sticking to what I thought was 'the only way', to show you that it is in fact, not.

So, I have decided at the age of six that I want to become a professional dancer with my *ultimate* goal of being the White Cat in Cats the Musical, on the West End. *That* will define my success and will *make* me happy. Six-year-old me is *100%* sure of it.

My value has been set and so unless I am performing as the White Cat in Cats the Musical on the West End in London, then *everything* else I *do* achieve in my life, will ultimately be seen as a failure in my eyes.

I then attend a local dance school until aged eighteen, move on to a professional Performing Arts College for three years, graduate and then…no West End job.

And actually, very few and far between auditions for Cats also.

As in, none.

So, now here I am, wondering what on Earth I'm going to do, because my dream isn't looking likely to come true and that's all I've ever wanted and what I *believe* is going to make me a successful dancer/human.

Skip a few years ahead with *lots* of super fun jobs and experiences being a dancer working all over the world under my belt, plus a *huge* mindset upgrade and inner strength like no other...then the realisations start to dawn on me.

1. I never would have been given the role of the White Cat when I left college, because I never *really* thought I deserved it, or believed I was capable of doing it. BOOM.
2. Everything that came my way, was *exactly* right for me at the time it came. SHAZAM.
3. There is always more than *one* way of doing something. AMEN.
4. Success lies in the eye of the beholder and whatever *they* believe to be true. MIC DROP.

Then skip a few more years ahead and here I am today. Writing a book about my experiences in dance and how to overcome anxiety, self-doubt and low confidence, so you can thrive.

And this isn't the first thing I've done that's made me walk *way* outside my conventional comfort zone line and it *won't* be the last.

When we see that in fact, there's a multitude of paths available to us that *each* involves incorporating what we most love doing, we are suddenly presented with *endless* possibilities, rather than a path filled with limiting road blocks.

In order for us to live fully, thrive wholly and reach our *true* potential, we must first work on creating new habits that mean we can sustain a life that we love.

If our mindset isn't in check, it doesn't matter how *badly* we want something, it just isn't on its way to us if we don't *truly* believe in our own abilities to receive it.

Take the example of me wanting that dream role in Cats. I wanted it a lot, there's no doubt about that. But because my self-belief and confidence were low, low, low, it wasn't going to happen for me.

In one way or another, I was unconsciously repelling away from me, the very thing I most wanted.

I put *all* my energy into doubting myself and my abilities and just didn't have room for all the love necessary to bring this dream into my reality.

I was surrounded by fear; fear of not being good enough mostly and ironically, this stopped me ever finding out if that fear-based belief was even true (which of course it wasn't and never is).

In a way, me *not* achieving this dream, was actually a blessing in disguise, because it taught me a lot about creating my own opportunities and work. It taught me to *make* things happen for myself and to think outside the box.

Because I *thought* that I had *no* control over the outcome of my success when other people had to decide it (for e.g. an audition panel) this actually spurred me on to find other ways to do what I loved in a way that I could never be rejected.

And that's when I properly became my own boss and started creating the work I wanted to do, instead of waiting for someone else to give it to me.

I started my own business, set up workshops and retreats all around the world, created my dance group 'Adelphi' and found the strength and courage to share my stories and lessons with others in the hope that it might help another person to feel happy, joyful, confident and empowered.

The fact of the matter is this; there are people out there experiencing life to the fullest, doing work *you'd* love to be doing and having the time of their lives whilst they're at it.

I'm not telling you this to evoke feelings of resentment or jealousy, no, I'm telling you this, because it means that *anything* is possible if we believe it is.

If you had told me when I was six years old, that I would end up dancing in Hong Kong, teaching in Norway, travelling the world solo, becoming my own boss and writing a book...I don't think I would have believed you, but now I *fully* believe that anything is up for grabs in this life.

So, just for this moment, forget *anything* you may have been told about limiting yourself in any way.

You, are limitless.

If there's a dream you want to achieve, you can.

If there's a burning inside you want to fulfil, you can.

Anything you can envision for yourself and your life, is possible.

Maybe life hasn't worked out the way you thought it would?

But that doesn't mean you can't change your current reality into something extraordinary!

If it's in your heart and you *really* believe that you deserve it and are capable of it, then *now* is the time to make an action plan so *you* can make *all* of your dreams come true.

Yes you, *you* can do that.

When that pesky little voice inside your head tries to convince you otherwise, ask it this simple question:

"Why *not* me?"

Those people in the world that are doing cool things and *#livingtheirbestlife* are incidentally, no different to you.

The only thing that *is* different in their life, is that they *decided* to make a life out of their living and created it *exactly* how they wanted it, with a whole load of self-belief behind the engine to keep the wheels turning.

It's easy to know what we don't want and even easier to *think* we know what we want, when the reality is, that more often than not, we've never really given ourselves the time and space to think about what gives us the most joy out of life.

Let alone go on to pursue that.

If you follow the usual path as a child, teenager and young adult, then there are no breaks that allow you space to daydream a little (except for that one glorious summer when you finish your GCSEs and have about ten months off to just, well, you know...hang around).

Now I'm not saying it's all playschool, school and more education, with no free time. All I'm saying is that, we can *think* we want something in life and make that our *one* and only focus, but not actually allow ourselves to explore the *many* other options and possibilities available to us that would bring us great joy too.

I knew I wanted to be a dancer. It's all I ever wanted to do, so my focus was on that.

And I *specifically* wanted to be the White Cat. It's all I'd ever wanted from age six, so my focus was *100%* on wanting that.

But I was also *super* young and hadn't experienced much of life or the world back then, so I didn't realise the abundance of other opportunities on offer as well.

I thought that being a dancer meant it was *this* job of being the White Cat, or nothing.

I'd either 'make it' (what does that even mean anyway?) or not. I was either going to realise my White Cat dream, or I wouldn't.

Looking back, I can see how limited I'd made my life by just solely focusing on that *one* dream and blocking a lot of really great ideas, opportunities and passions in the process.

Full disclosure: there is absolutely *nothing* wrong with having a dream like the one I have described. Or any dream that drives you daily.

All I'm saying, is that with hindsight, more worldly experience, a more flexible mindset and staying open to the magic, I am now able to follow the things I love without letting *fear* drive the car. I do what I love, *with* love.

Back then, I let fear drive me-I *needed* to realise that dream to prove to myself and others that I was good enough. I had to 'make it' otherwise it was all a waste. I was *desperate* to achieve my goal, or else I'd feel like a failure. Even though I didn't realise it at the time, there wasn't much love involved in my dream back then.

You see what I mean?

Whereas *now*, I create space, I follow the things I love and I don't analyse every, little thing. I know that everything I experience is for a reason and that it's *my* job to enjoy the journey. I realise that *I* can create whatever reality I want for myself. And I know that *my* opinion is the only one that truly matters in my life.

That doesn't mean that my dream was wrong.

What *wasn't* particularly working though, was acting out of fear and desperation with the *end* goal of me finally being happy, *rather* than enjoying every step on the journey. Which ultimately would have brought me happiness, love and self-belief and probably my dream job anyway.

Making a life out of your living involves you getting *really* clear on what you'd like your living to actually involve, how you'd like to spend your days, what makes you want to jump out of bed every morning and what sets your soul on fire. If that is to be a dancer, then get *really* specific on the details.

Get really clear on *that* stuff first. Don't overanalyse, just allow yourself to drift into a daydream and make the picture as detailed as possible.

When that voice inside you tries to question "How?", kindly reply with "I'll figure it all out".

If we already knew *how* to do everything, then what would be the point of this journey?

Half the fun is figuring out all the things you once didn't know how to do anyway.

From my own experience, focusing on the *how*, causes worry, doubt, anxiety and stress. Because sometimes our dreams can seem so far out of our reach and the journey to get there seems daunting and like a mountain we just don't want to climb.

When we follow the moments that feel good and keep doing the things we love, the *how* shows up naturally. But when we place our focus on the *how*, we live through worry, doubt and fear which actually pushes our dreams even further away from us.

I don't know about you, but I want to make a life out of my living whilst feeling fantastic! Not, make a life out of my living whilst feeling depleted and miserable.

When I was able to let go of what I *thought* I wanted and let go of all my expectations of the outcome or end result and instead focused on how I wanted to *feel* in each moment, what made my heart sing and what would add to my happiness on a daily basis, I felt free.

Free to choose, free to create and free to live on *my* terms.

This isn't about giving up on dreams, nor is it punishing yourself for following a certain path.

This is about *choosing* life work that really lights *you* up.

This is about realising your hearts desires and not feeling forced or pressurised to pursue something you realise you actually *don't* want.

This is about taking stock of your dreams and making sure they still fit you.

This is about following your heart by using love, not fear.

This is about knowing that *you* can create whatever reality you wish, as long as it's what you *truly* want, you really *believe* you can have it and your heart is fully in it.

It's so easy to see others' lives and think that *their* life defines what happiness *should* be and somehow, you're either doing it wrong, or not doing enough.

But when you take the time to make space for your heart to speak to you, it'll tell you everything you need to hear.

Then it's up to you to either follow it, follow someone else's heart path, or just do nothing and stay stuck in your uncertainty and fear.

It's the choice of struggling forward with fear, or moving effortlessly with love.

Nothing is right or wrong on a journey, but things can *feel* more aligned in your soul or not, so pay attention to how you're feeling regularly, so you can stay connected with yourself and keep course correcting if necessary.

Today, my dreams are a lot different to what they were when I was younger, mostly because I focus on how I want to *feel* in the present moment, *not* what I hope something will give me as an outcome after the event has happened.

If we're not happy right now, why will we be happy then?

It's time to start enjoying the *journey.*

Soul Love:

1. Write down what makes your heart soar, your face glow and your soul roar. Are you following that path? And if so, are you doing it with love or fear?

2. Let go of the *how*, let go of the expectation, let go full stop. Life is for living, not for fearing.

3. How do you want to feel in your life? Imagine waking up tomorrow, in a month, a year or in ten years...how do you want to *feel*?

CHAPTER 19

FOR THE LOVE OF DANCE

Do you remember why you started dancing?

I'm guessing you were quite a young little thing like I was, so perhaps the memory's a bit faded now?

Maybe you couldn't ever stand still, or kept trying to join in with your mum's home workout DVDs, or constantly jigged and danced about the house, persistently asking about going to dance class, until your parents finally (after two and a half years of life) enrolled you into lessons at your local dance school like I did!

Whatever your *why* was at the beginning, you carried on because of it.

Take a moment right now and think about *why* you dance?

Why do you love this artform so much?

What does it *give* you?

How do you *feel* inside your soul?

Having a passion, *I* think, is one of the most fantastic things you can experience as a human being.

The fire that burns inside your tummy, the pull you feel towards your chosen love and the fulfilment it gives you inside your soul as you engage with it.

I began dance lessons because I just couldn't stop moving when I was a child.

I think my parents were half reluctant to take me in case I *did* end up loving it and wanting to make it my career, as *all* they had heard were the whispers from the dance industry and they fully believed them back then.

But being the fabulous parents they are, they took me anyway.

And I loved it.

Of course.

When Billy Elliot came out on DVD years later, I was a mess of happy emotions.

For the first time in my life, someone had understood the way *I* felt about dance and put it into words that for so long, I could not.

Then they put those words to music and into a stage show on the West End and BOOM...fifteen shows and counting, tears galore and a very full heart is all I can say.

If you haven't seen the movie, then I may just have to order one off Amazon right now because, well, *where* have you been?

I relate to this story so much, not *just* because of the feelings Billy describes about his love of dance, but also because I *too* had started my dance career at my own Mrs Wilkinson dance school.

It wasn't County Durham, but it was near Hull and that's all I'm going to say about that!

In all fairness, my little village was a beautiful one, just outside the number one crap town as voted by Idler in 2003, with one tiny dance school which I attended for eight glorious years, making my family endure performances such as The Sound of Music where the Hull accent definitely added a certain *something* to the German wartime storyline...

My journey wasn't *exactly* like Billy's, but no two people's journeys are...mine was more like, The very hungry Caterpillar; except that the constant hunger *he* felt, was *my* constant hunger for outside validation and love and the copious amounts of food that *he* ate was actually the lessons and learnings *I* digested daily and the cocoon that *he* built for himself was really *my* dark tunnel of doom where I kept myself hidden...and the beautiful butterfly *he* revealed himself to be at the end was just the start of *my* beginning.

When The Greatest Showman came out in December 2017, I didn't really know much about it at the time because the Christmas festivities had taken over everything else (as they do *every* year in my family household).

So, I didn't realise just *how* much of an impact it would have on my life and career when I *did* finally watch it.

I had returned home at the end of January 2018 from co-hosting a brilliant retreat out in Bali with my wonderful friend, where I taught the dance and movement workshops and *all* I heard from my sister upon my return was how much I *needed* to go and see this film.

Now, my sister knows me *really* well-like, even more than I know myself sometimes, so I knew it *had* to be a corker if she was insisting I just *had* to go.

So, a few weeks later, we went. I wasn't sure what to expect and my sister had reassured me for the millionth time that it wasn't scary (all I'd seen was a circus type cover picture...I mean...clowns?!) and that I would absolutely love it.

She played a few of the songs on the drive to the cinema and it got me excited for what was to come.

Now don't worry, I'm not about to do a spoiler alert, so if you haven't seen it yet (again, where have you been?) then it's safe to keep reading.

But when that first note from the opening number hit my ears, I felt my whole body come alive. Even writing about it now is giving me Goosebumps!

I've been known to be a little bit of a Prima Donna/Drama Queen sometimes, exaggerating things for dramatic emphasis and all that Jazz, but what I'm telling you about this film is no exaggeration or overstatement.

From the very first note to the last, I had been on a journey like no other-all of my senses were wide awake, the love of dance and music coursing through my body and I felt so alive and free.

It was magical.

As we left the cinema (I didn't even try and hide my tears of joy) my sister turned to look at me with a face of pure knowing and she asked me what I thought.

I literally couldn't speak. Every time I tried to open my mouth and formulate words, my eyes filled up and my body felt like it was going to burst from adrenaline and undulated joy.

On the journey home, I sat in the passenger seat of the car, my mind swirling with ideas and inspiration, the sound of the musical score playing and the choreography.... Oh, the choreography!

From that night, my soul came alive once more.

I realised that I had been neglecting my passion for far too long and that a reaction *that* strong and intense could not be wrong, nor could it be ignored.

I knew then, that all the excuses or reasons I'd convinced myself about not working with my passion anymore just weren't true.

I was just, scared. Scared to put myself out there, scared of failing and scared that it wouldn't mean as much to me as it did before.

Well after that night's emotional display, I knew at least one of those fears could be struck off the list and that I just couldn't stop myself from doing what I loved so much anymore, no matter what ridiculous fears I'd been feeding myself with.

It was like Zeus himself had struck me that night...right in the heart with his lightning bolt, zapping me back to life for the second time.

When you find something you're passionate about, or maybe you feel like it's been part of you since birth like I do, no matter *how* hard you try to fight it, deny it or push it away, it has a sneaky way of showing up again and again until you finally pay attention and do something about it.

It can feel *really* scary to follow your dreams. Fear can, a lot of the time, stop you from even trying if you let it.

I know that I've let fear rule the roost before and I've also let love win. And life and everything in it, feels so much better when you live from the latter.

If you're struggling in life right now, just remember that there *is* a light and a way out of the tunnel. You just have to keep walking forward towards it every day.

Never give up hope, never give up on your dreams and *never* give up on yourself.

You need *you*.

The world needs *you*.

The more we do what we love, focus on the good, be grateful and live in the present moment, the better our lives (and our mental state) will be.

I know this to be true, because for so long all I could see was darkness. I never believed the light was there waiting for me if I just kept moving forward. I was stuck in my black tunnel of nothingness, just waiting, every day, for someone to come and pull me out.

When I realised that no one was coming in to get me, I slowly made my way through, straining to see the path, falling down a lot then scrambling back up and then slowly beginning to trust myself and hope that the light was still there, just around the next corner, to get me to the other side.

When we *aren't* filling ourselves up with the things that we love and that make our eyes fill with tears of joy, our hearts beat a little faster and our souls shine a little brighter, we can feel utterly depleted and empty inside.

Depression, anxiety or any other negative emotion is how we label those feelings of nothingness.

And when we first fall into our tunnel, it can be hard to get the strength to find a way out again.

But when we start putting lots of good things in, things like gratitude, joy, hope, passion, peace, connection and love, we give ourselves the tools to carve a new path towards our freedom at the end of the darkness.

This is why it's *so* important to do the things you love in life.

My passion was (and always will be) dancing and yet, at the time when I *really* felt my worst, I wasn't doing that. I was missing out on every good feeling I knew it would give me because I was scared, because I let fear reign supreme and because I felt just too depressed and anxious to even try.

But sometimes you have to *make* yourself get *really* uncomfortable and do the things you just don't want to do, in order to get everything you've ever wanted.

The more I engaged in activities I loved doing; things like dancing, teaching, writing, learning, connecting with friends, being with family, reading, taking baths, going to cafes, booking trips, laughing, watching movies, being in the sunshine, working on my business...the more I felt like me again.

I used to think "I'll be happy when...when I get that job, when I'm noticed in class, when I have a boyfriend, when I travel abroad, when I live here, there, do this or that etc".

I really believed that "When..." would bring me everything I was searching for.

I *honestly* thought that when I got to "When..." *everything* would all fall into place and I'd *finally* be happy and feel at peace.

But like so many people do, I was trying to work from the outside in.

I put all my happiness and good feelings outside of myself.

And when "When..." arrived and I *still* wasn't happy, I wondered what on earth was wrong with my theory...and *me*.

When I finally, *finally* (I put in two for extra emphasis because it took *that* long) realised that in order to be happy, I needed to work from the inside out, I began to experience happiness and joy like I'd never felt before.

Because when I started doing this-filling up my cup with all the good thoughts, the good emotions and the things that I loved, I found that I was already happy, in that very moment.

This lightened the load a *whole* bunch! Really.

It meant I didn't have to *wait* for happiness any longer-I could feel it whenever I wanted to, along with every other positive emotion.

And that in turn, meant that all my negative emotions were then overridden by the positive ones and life got a *lot* lighter *and* brighter, because my tunnel had started to fade away behind me.

Dance has been like a third parent to me; always there no matter what, providing a stable home I can always come back to, nurturing me to be my best and lovingly challenging me to push myself beyond what I ever thought was possible, helping me to spread my wings and find freedom of my own, being a true friend, a mentor and the biggest and best gift of all…giving me life.

Whatever your dreams are for yourself and your life, just know that everything you're thinking *can* become your reality.

You already have everything you'll ever need right now.

The person who is going to make all your dreams come true is the person standing in front of the mirror looking back at you each day.

You can *be* whatever you choose to be.

You can *do* whatever you want to do.

You can *have* whatever you want to have.

No exceptions.

Really, believe me when I say, *anything* is possible.

Before I finish, I want to tell you just a few real truths that might come in handy whilst you're on this journey we call life and they are as follows...

1. You are *never* too old
2. It is *never* too late
3. It'll *never* be the 'right' time
4. Everything you are looking for is inside you already
5. *You* create your own reality, no one else
6. If you have a dream, go and live it. NOW!
7. Life really is short and if it's not life or death, it's not *that* serious, so laugh a little more!
8. Be with people you love
9. Spend time alone and get to know yourself (even though it might feel scary at first)
10. Focus on the good and remain grateful throughout everything
11. Move your body and take care of the temple you live in
12. Life is a reflection, look closely
13. Don't take things *so* personally...it's *never* about you
14. Remember *why* you started and do it for the love of doing it
15. Make your *own* rules and create your *own* beliefs that serve you
16. *Nothing* is out of your reach
17. Don't deny your passions-answer the call inside you, otherwise it will just keep ringing louder
18. Believe in yourself *first*

19. Breathe
20. Love yourself and make *you* your No.1 priority every
    day for the rest of your life

Soul Love:

1. What makes *your* soul come alive? Make a list of everything that lights you up.

2. Work out how often you are currently doing these things and how you would feel if you added more of them into your daily life.

3. Start filling up your soul with all of those good things as often as you can and continue to listen to your intuition and what you *really* need to be your best self.

CHAPTER 20

FORGIVE AND LET GO

*"Holding on to anger is like grasping
a hot coal with the intent of throwing
it at someone else; you are the
one who gets burned"*
-Buddha

When we feel that someone has wronged us or an injustice has been made, it is easy to hold a grudge or feel anger towards our wrongdoers.

But Buddha was spot on when he said this, because despite the false benefits that holding on to anger, pain, resentment or frustration can give us, we can never *really* be happy until we learn to let go of them.

Letting go (along with learning to be my own best friend) has probably been my biggest lesson so far.

When I left college, I left with three years of *extraordinary* technical training, a handful of amazing friends and a suitcase bursting to the brim with grudges, anger, resentment and pain.

Those three years at dance college pushed me beyond what I ever thought I was capable of doing; physically, emotionally and mentally.

I experienced some of the strongest emotions I'd ever felt, like anger, frustration, despair, anxiety and depression and I blamed them *all* on outside forces and people.

I believed that college and certain individuals had caused me to feel the way I was feeling. Like they had actually *made* me feel such sadness and pain.

I was *so* sure that dispelling these emotions was out of my control and that my happiness in fact, relied on outer circumstances and people *making* me feel happy 24/7.

I carried these emotions around in my overflowing suitcase for *years*.

Never forgiving all the people and events that had wronged me or caused me pain in some way and constantly bringing these negative emotions with me *wherever* I went, in *whatever* I did.

I felt that by me holding on to these negative emotions, I was justifying myself, because it meant that *they* (whoever 'they' were; college in general, specific people, audition panels etc) were in the wrong and me struggling at life was just the *proof* to show that what *they* did to me was so horrible and unjust.

By remaining and actively choosing to live in this constant state of fear-based emotions, I was proving my point not only to myself, but also to those around me, that I had been hurt unfairly and I couldn't *possibly* recover from that pain because it just wasn't acceptable as I had convinced myself and I needed other people to know that too.

But in thinking this way, I was actually just *prolonging* my hurt and pain, reliving past events and bringing all of that negative emotion to the surface and feeling bitter and resentful for 'what *they* did to me' all those years ago.

If I had learned to forgive early on and experienced just how freeing this act would be, I would have realised that by doing so, it didn't mean that I *approved* of the wrong doings or unjust behaviour of others towards myself, it just simply meant that I could *choose* to no longer let it affect me and as a glorious result, finally release myself and experience true freedom and peace of mind.

But sadly, I did *not* realise this life changing fact until many years later, after which I had endured countless years of (subconsciously choosing) pain, sadness and struggle.

When someone says something *not* so nice to our face, behind our back, live on TV or even in a comment on Instagram, this can disrupt our peace very easily if we let it.

We may even find that we harbour a grudge for a while and feel sad and annoyed that they could even *say* such a thing, when it simply just isn't true!

We may *also* put that person on our 'Naughty List' and remove them from all further Christmas cards as a way of punishment.

All of these responses are keeping us in a negative state.

Meanwhile, the other person doesn't give two hoots about the thoughts going on in your head or how you're still thinking about that thing they said to you two years ago, because they're just getting on with their own life.

So again, Buddha is right.

However, if we decide that what *we* know to be true about ourselves is *all* we need to know and believe, then this negative comment may make us sit up and think 'Huh?' but then we can quickly decide to just LET IT GO.

We would then avoid the unnecessary pain and no one could *ever* disturb our peace again.

We would be choosing the loving option *for ourselves, not* for the other person.

Ultimately, we let go so we can feel free from whatever we believe is taking away our peace and joy.

I know full well that holding on to anger can create nasty things in our bodies and minds and at the end of the day, it's all self-inflicted…because at any time, we can *choose* to forgive and let go.

During my time at college and into my early twenties, I let *every* mean comment, criticism and 'unfair' circumstance seep into my very core and stay there.

I held on to that hot coal so tightly, constantly burning myself as a result, never realising that the one simple thing to stop all of my pain and suffering, would be to just forgive and let go of the hot coal.

Now, forgiveness does not just apply to other people that have wronged us.

It also applies to ourselves and this can sometimes be an *even* harder task to take part in.

The way we speak to ourselves, can be, quite frankly, awful!

Take a moment to think about some of the things you say to yourself on the regular-things that are being etched into your subconscious-things that will stay with you throughout your life, unless you change them…

Not nice right?

Now imagine saying them out loud so other people can hear them too.

Cringe! Anyone fancy climbing into this hole with me?

Now imagine saying these things to your very best friend or your mum.

Not cool, would you agree?

So why in the hell do we say these things to ourselves!!!

Madness.

Maybe it's time we all started being nicer, kinder and more loving towards ourselves?

Maybe it's time to forgive and let go of every, little thing we believe we've done wrong?

Maybe it's just time.

Sometimes we make little mistakes. Sometimes we mess up a lot.

And sometimes we don't remember that we're only human and these things are just a normal part of *everyone's* life.

The really, super, duper important thing to do, is to forgive yourself *anyway* and LET IT GO.

We cannot change the past, nor control the future, but what we *can* do, is be the happiest version of ourselves in the present moment and to do that, we must learn to let go of anything keeping us stuck or in pain.

I remember when I tried to persist in holding on to negative things from the past so much that the signs I got from the Universe that followed, were so *hilariously* obvious, it was like a big ol' slap in the face.

I'm not joking.

I'd hear songs on the radio about letting go as I drove in my car, open a book to the exact page about letting go, overhear conversations of people nearby at cafes talking about this very subject, read emails, have Instagram posts pop up and see signs in the street about this very thing-all whilst trying to subconsciously push it away from me.

There's a great quote that sums up what I was doing at this time:

"What you resist, persists"
-Carl Jung

And the one that made me stop in my tracks and *finally* surrender to the Universe's bigger plan, was when I was on a swing in Bali.

I'd been going through some various different life struggles at that time, trying to make sense of both my personal and professional life and remember *who* I was and just *what* I wanted out of life.

I took some time to figure this out and even though I was getting there and starting to make sense of it all, there was still a part of me that was holding on to something and I just *couldn't* seem to let it go.

I didn't know what it was, but all I knew was that it was keeping me from fully moving forward.

So, after taking a little time out for myself, the day came for me to once again pack my bags and head to Bali, to meet my amazing friend/co-host and welcome the ladies attending our second retreat.

I was *really* excited and much less afraid to fly solo across the world this time after doing it once already earlier in the year. I had exciting classes planned for the ladies and I *knew* that I had something of value to share with them.

And yet still, there was something inside me that was trying to resist, something that was holding me back, something that I couldn't let go of. I just didn't know what on *earth* it was.

When I arrived in Bali, I met my friend and we set off to our first villa to plot and plan an amazing five days for the ladies coming, get adjusted to the time zone (and climate) and generally have a catch up and enjoy the delicious food available to us.

The retreat was *more* than I could have hoped for and the group we had bonded like they were all long lost sisters. It was such a magical atmosphere to witness and I loved every minute of it.

After we said our goodbyes at the end of the week, my friend and I decided to stay a little longer to explore the island and basically, have a bit of a holiday.

We had both said things that we'd like to do (luckily, eating yummy food was top of the list for both of us) and so we worked our way through the list, ticking things off and having a lot of fun along the way.

All the while, there was *still* something in the back of my mind that wouldn't seem to quit. It was becoming a bit of a nuisance to be quite honest.

On one of our last days together, I suggested we try out this really cool and *really* high swing.

I now actually enjoy pushing myself out of my comfort zone because I know it's good for me and I know that I'll get a rush after accomplishing the thing I was originally scared to do. But oftentimes I agree to things wholeheartedly *before* fully thinking it through and realising what it actually entails, because I've just seen a great brochure advertising a lot of happy, smiley people doing the thing I want to try and being sold on that (hello sucker for advertising!).

So, I was fully up for this swing (and before you think I'm being a baby-Google it!) excited to try something new and have some fun.

But when we walked inside the place and I saw the swings in real life, how high they *actually* were and the screams of the people *on* them, something began to stir in my tummy and chest and I started having second thoughts at the same time as opening my mouth and *agreeing* to do the 'Extreme Swing' with my friend.

It was all a bit of a blur from that point on.

But there we were, tickets in hand, heading towards the highest swing, me trying and failing to act cool and nonchalant in front of my *very* cool and calm friend.

As we were getting kitted up (standing on the edge of the hill drop...*this* is health and safety in Bali!) my heart was pounding, my legs were trembling and my mind was whirring with all the 'What if' fears I thought I had quietened.

We sat next to each other in the swing; me, a total nervous wreck and my friend, well cooler than a cucumber in the fridge and I regrettably said to the guys around us *not* to push us too hard because I was frightened...so what does that translate to? It doesn't matter what language is being spoken, if you're afraid, this just fuels the fire.

They pulled the swing back (there were at least four of them-this is how big a deal this swing was alright!) my hands gripped tightly to the bar and my friend's back, whilst she was *all* smiles and had a visibly normal breathing rate that I envied.

When they let us go, I'm not even sure what noise came out of my mouth in that moment.

It was, I think, pure terror.

And we had fourteen more swings to go!

Each time, they would push us a little higher and every time I thought my poor thumping heart would suddenly leap out of my chest and fall to the ground just to escape the horror.

After about six or seven goes, I heard the guys who were pushing us shout something from below us as our legs almost touched the sky, but I couldn't make out what it was because all my concentration was focused on gripping, holding my breath or screaming.

When my friend let her hand go from the side bar, I was in total shock. I managed to turn slightly towards her mid swing and ask what the hell she was doing and then the words of the guys below rang out like a foghorn.

"LET GO".

They were *all* shouting it. And they were shouting it, to *me*.

At first, I tried to ignore them, then I tried to convince myself of how ludicrous their command was and then...then I had a realisation.

Their call was *so* loud in my ears, it was *all* I could hear and *all* I could focus on.

This sign, whether from God, the Universe or simply from four frustrated Balinese men, was the sign I was *ready* to listen to.

I was *totally* out of my comfort zone, in the middle of what I can only describe as a near death experience, listening for the first time to the one thing I had closed my ears to for so long.

I laughed inside and gave a teeny, tiny smile to the Universe to let it know I had heard the call.

And in that moment, I slowly began to uncurl my claw like fingers from around the bar and reached my arm into the unknown, fearing that *this* would be the very moment I fell and plummeted to my death, but deciding to trust in myself and do it anyway.

I've only been *that* scared one other time in my life and actually looking back on the event now, I'm pretty sure *that* was my hurdle to overcome and learn this lesson of letting go, but I didn't learn it then, so of course, it decided to show up at the death swing instead.

Talk about not picking a safe and cosy learning moment Universe!

But this is what I *needed* and what it had come to for me to *actually* pay attention.

Even though my whole being was crying out *not* to let go, I did it anyway and after the initial fear of falling and dying was safely out of the way, I began to feel the air rushing past me, the beautiful view that I'd missed out on for about eleven swings and finally felt, free.

When we resist the lessons we *need* to learn in life, they just keep on coming, or in my case, they keep on shouting at you like the Balinese men did to me.

I hadn't realised just *how* much I was still holding on to from past pain and suffering even then. I thought I'd managed to work through my 'stuff', but sometimes the Universe knows better than we do and we just *have* to listen to it and again, let it *all* go.

From that moment, I consciously made the choice to forgive and let go. Let go of everything I had been trying to control, let go of my grip on life, let go of my past hurt and pain and finally breathe life in instead.

I wanted my freedom *more* than I wanted to be right in my stubbornness of suffering, so I stepped into the unknown and came out the other side swinging.

Even though you might not believe the person, event or circumstance who did you wrong deserves your forgiveness, give them it anyway.

Forgive them anyway, so *you* can move on.

Forgive them anyway, so *you* can forgo the pain and suffering.

Forgive them anyway and *let it go*.

Value your peace of mind, your health, your happiness and your joy, *more* than valuing your injustice and being right.

The past is gone and we cannot change it.

But the present moment *and* your future is still up for grabs and only *you* get to decide how that plays out.

Will you choose happiness and joy for yourself?

Or will you hold on to the hot coal?

The choice is always yours.

Make it count.

Mind, Body, Soul Love:

1. Choose love over fear

2. Choose forgiveness

3. Choose to let go

RESOURCES

WHEN YOU NEED A HELPING HAND

I believe that we will *never* be done learning, growing or evolving.

What would be the point of life if we reached our full potential, learned every lesson and had it all sorted by the age of twelve or even seventy for that matter?

When I got my Degree at age twenty one, I vowed I would *never* do any more education ever again (this actually makes me laugh out loud at the ridiculousness of twenty one year old me, but okay, I get it, dissertations are hard) but this went right out of the window and thank goodness, as I went on to *overachieve* in the way of higher education, personal development and emotional healing and learned more than I ever thought my little brain could.

If you're going through a struggle right now like I did, then I'd like to pass on some things that have helped me to feel better on my journey so far and given me hope, joy and peace as a result.

I hope they can provide you with some sense of relief as well and inspire you to do more of the things that make *you* feel good.

Sometimes, we just want to feel better and everything on my list has done that for me. They're personal to me for my *own* journey, but they may just end up being something that helps *you* to feel better too.

Take what you will for yourself and add as many as you like to your own list of resources, so maybe one day very soon, *you* can pass them along to someone else who might need them.

Some on the list may be obvious, others may not, some you might think are fitting to the theme of this book, others you may think are completely random, but I'd like to point out that things don't necessarily have to make sense for you to get a positive benefit from them.

Everything I've listed is for a reason...they've helped me on my healing journey in some way or another; whether that was to inspire, reassure, excite my senses, instil positivity, give me strength of mind and resilience, light a fire inside, bring joy, create positive habits and thoughts, have a calming influence, help to find inner peace or to simply make me laugh (which of course we all know, is the *best* medicine around).

I know you have the power and potential already inside you to become the very best version of *you* possible, you just have to believe it for yourself too.

RESOURCES:

Books: The Alchemist by Paulo Coelho, The Big Leap by Gay Hendricks, The Undomestic Goddess by Sophie Kinsella, The girl with the pearl earring by Tracy Chevalier, The Secret by Rhonda Byrne, The Sound of Laughter by Peter Kay, Darcey Bussell's Autobiography, Feel the fear and do it anyway by Susan Jeffers, Man's search for meaning by Viktor E. Frankl, Confessions of Georgia Nicholson series by Louise Rennison, The Success Principles by Jack Canfield, Girl Boss by Sophia Amoruso

Musicals: Cats, Billy Elliot, Thriller LIVE, Frozen (On Broadway), Starlight Express, Our House, Shrek, Kinky Boots, How to succeed at business without really trying, Promises Promises

Films: Billy Elliot, The Greatest Showman, Honey, Step Up, Moana, Eddie the Eagle, Rocky, My Big Fat Greek Wedding, It's a Wonderful Life, The Pursuit of Happyness, I Feel Pretty

TV Series: Friends, Will & Grace, Sex and the City, Ugly Betty, Modern Family, 50 ways to kill your Mammy, The Unbreakable Kimmy Schmidt, An Idiot Abroad

Podcasts: Get Merry Podcast by The Merrymaker Sisters, The Marie Forleo Podcast, The Ricky Gervais Show

YouTube: TED talks, Tony Robbins, Tara Stiles Strala Yoga, Marie Forleo

Audiobooks: Subliminal Mastery Series: Self Esteem by Louise L. Hay, You are a Badass/You are a Badass at making money by Jen Sincero, The Power by Rhonda Byrne, Hungry For More by Mel Wells

Public Figures: Arnold Schwarzenegger, Misty Copeland, Sylvester Stallone, Deliciously Ella (if you're in London, get yourself to her Deli ASAP), Will Smith, Darcey Bussell, Bobby Newberry, Tara Stiles, Hugh Jackman

Places: New York City-USA, Tromso-Norway, Mykonos-Greece, Hong Kong-China, St.Petersburg and Moscow-Russia, Las Vegas-USA, Tokyo-Japan, Melbourne-Australia, Bali-Indonesia, Phuket-Thailand, Berlin-Germany, Los Angeles-USA, Reykjavik-Iceland

Movement: Dancing, Mat Pilates, Reformer Pilates, Strala Yoga, Swimming and Walking (especially in nature)

If you'd like to continue with your personal and professional development or need some more guidance, here are some useful links that I can highly recommend:

NLP training:

https://www.centreofexcellence.com/

Personal Training/Fitness Qualifications:

https://www.premierglobal.co.uk/
https://www.hfe.co.uk/

Strala Yoga Trainings:

http://stralayoga.com/

International Student Visa Program at Broadway Dance Center:

https://www.broadwaydancecenter.com/

Mental Health Information:

https://www.mind.org.uk/

ACKNOWLEDGEMENTS

Firstly, I would like to say the biggest thank you to my family, especially my wonderful parents and sister and my loving partner John for always believing in me, supporting me throughout everything and always encouraging me to go for my dreams. Thank you for the unconditional love, always.

Thank you to my two nieces who continue to teach me more than they will ever know.

A big thank you to all my mentors over the years; Chio, Brian Nicholson, David Leighton, Norma Terry, Tara Stiles, Mel Wells and Debbie Watt. You have all inspired me to be the best I can be.

A massive shout out to my wonderful tribe of friends (you know who you are!) who have stuck by me all these years. Thank you to each of you for being so wonderful and weird and for all of the laughter and fun you've brought to my life.

A great big thank you to Sean Patrick, my publisher for all the help, belief and support and for the Universe bringing us together at just the right time!

Thank you to all my teachers who have passed on their knowledge to me, especially Miss Lynn Gay (where it all began) and to all my students over the years who have trusted me to do the same.

Huge thanks to Hayley Richardson, Felicity West, Kamran Bedi and Peter Watkins for their creativity, advice and support.

And one final shout out to you, the reader. Thank you for picking up this book and for wanting to be the best version of you possible.

ABOUT THE AUTHOR

Emily Sophie is an experienced dance and fitness professional, Strala Yoga Guide and NLP Practitioner.

She teaches classes, workshops and hosts retreats all around the world as well as having programmes available online on her website.

She is also the Founder/Choreographer of her dance group 'Adelphi'.

Emily believes that finding movement that feels good and that we enjoy, creating a strong, positive mindset and practicing self-love daily will enable a happy, healthy life and aims to spread this message in all that she does.

To find out more about Emily and her services, please see below:

Web: www.emilysophie.co.uk

Instagram: @iamemilysophie @adelphi_dance_group

Facebook: facebook.com/iamemilysophie

9 781912 779642